PARTISANS AND REDCOATS

ALSO BY WALTER EDGAR

South Carolina: A History

South Carolina in the Modern Age

PARTISANS AND REDCOATS

The Southern Conflict That Turned the Tide of the American Revolution

WALTER EDGAR

WILLIAM MORROW • 75 YEARS OF PUBLISHING
An Imprint of HarperCollins*Publishers*

HarperCollins books may be purchased for educational, business,
or sales promotional use.
For information please write: Special Markets Department,
HarperCollins Publishers Inc., 10 East 53rd Street, New York, NY 10022.

FIRST EDITION

Designed by Kate Nichols

Printed on acid-free paper

Library of Congress Cataloging-in-Publication Data

Edgar, Walter B., 1943–
Partisans and Redcoats : the Southern Conflict that turned the tide
of the American Revolution /
Walter Edgar.—1st ed.
p.   cm.
Includes bibliographical references and index.
ISBN 0-380-97760-5 (acid-free paper)
1. South Carolina—History—Revolution, 1775–1783.   2. South
Carolina—History—Revolution, 1775–1783—Biography.   3. South
Carolina—History—Revolution, 1775–1783—Social aspects.   4. United
States—History–Revolution, 1775–1783—Biography.   5. United
States—History—Revolution, 1775–1783—Social aspects.   I. Title.

E263.S7 E38   2001
973.3'092'2—dc21
00-069722

01   02   03   04   05   QW   10   9   8   7   6   5   4   3   2   1

For

my mother and my father

CONTENTS

ACKNOWLEDGMENTS

———•———

The American Revolution in the South Carolina backcountry is a subject in which I have long been interested. I am grateful to William Morrow for giving me the opportunity to write this little book about a series of events and people often overlooked in more traditional histories.

In my research, Sam Thomas of the York County Cultural and Heritage Commission was most cooperative. His walking tour of the site of the Battle of Huck's Defeat was a morning well spent. Jennifer Bean of the Museum of Early Southern Decorative Arts in Winston-Salem, North Carolina, once again came up with a needed illustration. Eric Stevens of the Department of Geography at the University of South Carolina drew the maps. As always, Allen Stokes and his wonderful staff at the South Caroliniana Library—especially Beth Bilderback and Robin Copp, Thelma Hayes, and Mark Herro—answered every demand I made on them. Sandra Powers of the library at Anderson House of the Society of the Cincinnati checked several resources. Rhett Jackson, Paul MacKenzie, and Jim Hammond read the manuscript and offered suggestions. Alex Moore prepared the index. My friend Mark Smith always had an encouraging word. My wife, Betty, made sure that I kept to my schedule to complete the manuscript on time. I dedicate this book to Amelia Moore Edgar and Charles Ernest Edgar Jr., my late mother and my father, who first introduced me to the world of Revolutionary America.

Walter Edgar
Columbia, South Carolina

INTRODUCTION

America's First Civil War: The South Carolina Backcountry, 1775–1782

For they sow the wind, and they shall reap the whirlwind.
HOSEA 8:7

On the eve of the American Revolution, South Carolina was the wealthiest colony in British North America. The aggregate wealth of inventoried estates in Charleston was more than six times that of Philadelphia.[1] Charleston, one of the five great cities of colonial America, was the social, economic, and political capital of the colony. The elite who controlled South Carolina owed their wealth to rice, indigo, and the labor of thousands of black slaves. In 1775 there were 104,000 black Carolinians, but only 70,000 whites. Of these whites, nearly two-thirds (approximately 46,000) lived in what was called the backcountry.

The South Carolina backcountry began about fifty miles inland and stretched to the foothills of the Appalachians. Until the 1730s, this vast area was populated mainly by Catawba and Cherokee Indians. At first only a handful of settlers, many of them German, Welsh, and Scots-Irish, ventured into the interior of the colony. Then, in the 1740s and 1750s, hundreds of settlers poured into the Carolina backcountry via the Great Wagon Road that ran from Pennsylvania through the Shenandoah Valley of Virginia to the Savannah River Valley along the border between South Carolina and Georgia.

A majority of these new arrivals were Scots-Irish, but a fair number were English and German. They laid claim to lands that had for centuries belonged to Native Americans. In 1760 the Cherokee, urged on by the French, launched an attack on the frontier settlements. In a panic, frontier families abandoned their homes for the safety of scattered forts. With the assistance of British troops, South Carolina eventually was able to defeat the Cherokee.

Although the Indians were pushed into the extreme western portion of the colony, the troubles had not ended for the men and women who were trying to carve their homes out of the wilderness. The Cherokee War had rent the fragile fabric of frontier society and attracted lawless individuals from other colonies. In 1766 and 1767, outlaws and bandits terrorized the law-abiding residents of the backcountry. No one, regardless of age or gender, was safe from their depredations.

Appeals to the colonial authorities in Charleston went unheeded. In desperation, those who had a stake in society formed a vigilante movement and called themselves Regulators—they were going to regulate society, create law and order. However, the Regulators went beyond ridding the backcountry of thieves and brigands. They also took it upon themselves to discipline those they termed "the lower sort," and they sowed the seeds for internal conflict that would later bear bitter fruit.

No sooner had the frontier begun to calm down than a heated

constitutional dispute between the colonial assembly and imperial officials led to a government shutdown. After 1771, for all practical purposes, royal government ceased in South Carolina. Over the next four years, a number of extralegal organizations came into existence that eventually became the independent government of South Carolina.

The revolutionaries (or patriots, as they were beginning to call themselves) controlled Charleston and the lowcountry, but not much else. In the backcountry, there were individuals who had greater grievances with the South Carolina Commons House of Assembly than with the British Parliament. The patriots were in a quandary. With the large black majority in the lowcountry, they desperately needed the support of backcountry whites—a number of whom were loyalists—friends of the king (or as patriots derisively termed them, Tories). Initially the revolutionaries obtained a grudging pledge of neutrality from prominent backcountry leaders. Then, late in 1775, patriots imprisoned leading backcountry Tories, and in response, Tory militia units attacked patriot troops. In savage fighting that would presage the brutal nature of the American Revolution in South Carolina, the Tory uprising was suppressed.

During the first seven months of 1776, the revolutionary forces of South Carolina defeated a British task force at the Battle of Sullivan's Island and the Cherokee on the frontier. By the end of the year, an unnatural calm, not unlike that of the calm before a hurricane, had descended upon the state. Charleston Harbor bustled with shipping. In the backcountry, many opted to farm and build up their holdings rather than join the army. The danger from Great Britain seemed far away.

In 1778 British forces captured Savannah and invaded South Carolina. Although repulsed, they returned in 1780 and captured Charleston. Thinking all was lost, commanders of forts in the interior surrendered to the British. As they set about securing what they now considered a conquered province, the British and their loyalist allies committed numerous atrocities. They took civilians as hostages; they wantonly and unlawfully destroyed and appropriated property not justified by military necessity; they deprived prisoners of war and civilians of the right of fair trials; they compelled prisoners of war and civilians to serve in the forces of a hostile power; they unlawfully confined civilians; they destroyed and willfully damaged institutions dedicated to religion; they plundered public and private property. And, against a civilian population, they committed torture, imprisonment, murder, and "other inhumane acts." If these actions had been committed in the 1990s instead of the 1780s, Lord Cornwallis and a number of his subordinates, such as Banastre Tarleton and James Wemyss, would have been indicated by the International Tribunal at the Hague as war criminals.[2]

From Charles, Lord Cornwallis, to the humblest Tory militiaman, the occupying forces believed that fear and brutality would cow the populace. Instead, the strategy backfired. Partisan bands led by Thomas Sumter, Francis Marion, and others arose to fight the British at every turn. Cornwallis's grand plan of rolling up the Carolinas to Virginia began to unravel in the backcountry of South Carolina.

During the month of July 1780, there were at least eight battles in the backcountry. In the months to follow, there were eleven more, all leading up to the Battle of King's Mountain. Of all these battles, Huck's Defeat was the most significant. It was the first British setback since the capitulation of Charleston, and it gave hope to those who wished to resist the British army of occupation.

Even the name Huck's Defeat suggests the nature of the fighting in the backcountry. Captain Christian Huck's forces burned homes, shot unarmed men, and threatened women. Their actions roused the countryside and led to their defeat on 12 July 1780. The Battle of Huck's Defeat is a story of wanton cruelty and heroism, of the fierce devotion of both patriots and Tories to their respective causes, of women who were unafraid to act to protect their homes and loved ones, and of a dash of chivalry that somehow survived in the maelstrom of the civil war in the South Carolina backcountry.

For while South Carolinians were fighting the British army, they were also fighting one another. There were no rules, no Geneva Convention. Neighbors killed neighbors, and fathers turned on sons. Trusting one's brother could be fatal. The only thing a man could trust was his best friend, his rifle.

Many of the atrocities—and *atrocity* is not too strong a word—committed in the civil war in South Carolina were initiated by British regulars or their Tory allies. Patriot militia bands responded in kind, and the violence escalated into a fury that laid waste to entire communities.[3]

"South Carolina," wrote the nineteenth-century historian George Bancroft, "moved toward independence through the bitterest afflictions of civil war. . . . Families were divided; patriots outlawed and savagely assassinated; houses burned, and women and children driven into the forests; districts so desolated that they seemed the abode only of orphans and widows."[4]

The British policy was coldly deliberate. "[I]n a civil war," wrote Lord Cornwallis, "there is no admitting of neutral characteristics, and . . . those who are not clearly with us must so far be considered against us." Cornwallis and the British did not realize that they were pursuing a policy that was counterproductive. "Brutality, fear, and the resultant social disorganization can work only for the guerrillas, no matter who initiates them."[5] Nowhere was that more true than in the South Carolina backcountry.

The rising of the South Carolina backcountry to fight the

British was a momentous occurrence in the American Revolution. The Battle of Huck's Defeat and the other engagements in the summer and fall of 1780 were the turning of the tide in the American Revolution in the South. Every British soldier lost was a soldier who could not be replaced. As the patriot bands stepped up their activities, the Tories became more desperate. Their depredations led to an escalation of the civil strife that caused more backcountry folk to choose the cause of liberty. It was a desperate struggle.

The American Revolution was won in the South by determined backcountry patriots. Some, such as Andrew Pickens and Thomas Sumter, became American folk heroes. This book tells the story, however, of relatively unknown men and women, such as William and Martha Bratton, Watt, Joseph Kerr, Mary McClure, William Hill, and William Martin, who were willing to risk their lives for the cause of American liberty. Their courage, sacrifice, and resistance during the summer and fall of 1780 were the first steps on the road to King's Mountain, Cowpens, Guilford Courthouse, Yorktown—and victory.

PARTISANS AND REDCOATS

1

The South Carolina Backcountry: Taming the Southern Frontier

―――・―――

This is a very fruitful Spot, thro' which the dividing Line between North and South Carolina runs—The Heads of P. D. [Pee Dee] River, Lynch's Creek, and many other Creeks take their Rise in this Quarter—so that a finer Body of Land is no where to be seen—But it is occupied by a Sett of the most lowest vilest Crew breathing—Scotch Irish Presbyterians from the North of Ireland.

REVEREND CHARLES WOODMASON, 25 JANUARY 1767

The "fruitful Spot" described by the itinerant Anglican missionary Charles Woodmason was the Waxhaws, a settlement along the border between the colonies of North and South Carolina. To Woodmason's friends in Charleston, the Waxhaws might as well have been on another planet. To the incredibly wealthy members of the South Carolina elite, the only world that mattered was their own—the fabled Carolina lowcountry—and it ended about fifty miles from the coast. In the lowcountry parish of St. George Dorchester was a crossroads called

Parish End. The name said it all, except that it might have been more appropriately called World's End. The rest of the colony was dismissively referred to as the backcountry.[1]

Much of the backcountry lay in the South Carolina pied-mont—a land of rolling hills and lush valleys. The topsoil was rich, but it was only about twelve inches deep in most places, and beneath it was red clay. The forests were predominantly oak and hickory with a scattering of pine and gum trees. Dogwood, red maple, and spice bush were the understory trees. In low-lying areas, were dense canebrakes. In the springtime, native azaleas, buttercups, honeysuckle, Indian pinks, trillium, iris, and violets brightened the fields and forests.[2]

Dozens of streams of all sizes rived the land, creating the val-leys to which early settlers were drawn. Although many of these creeks and rivers began as crystal-clear mountain rivulets, they were soon clouded by soil and vegetable matter.[3]

In the fields and forests could be found all sorts of wild game: beavers, deer, turkeys, quail, rabbits, opossums, raccoons, bears, foxes, squirrels, wolves, geese, and ducks. In the streams were trout, bream, and catfish. Flocks of passenger pigeons darkened the sky, and the howls of panthers could still be heard. Until the middle of the eighteenth century, when European settlement eliminated them, buffalo still roamed. Ironically, it was the buffalo runs or paths, transformed into trading routes by Indians and Europeans, that became the highways that helped open up the backcountry to settlers.[4]

In 1740 there were very few Europeans in the South Carolina backcountry. By the American Revolution, nearly one-half of the colony's total population, and 80 percent of its white population, lived there.[5]

The migration of predominantly Scots-Irish settlers trans-formed the lower South and, in the final analysis, was key to

America's triumph over Great Britain in the Revolution. The Great Wagon Road that served as the settlers' highway began across the Schuylkill River from Philadelphia. From the Pennsylvania capital it went west to Harrisburg and then turned south, following the great Shenandoah Valley through Maryland and Virginia into the piedmont of North Carolina. The road veered slightly southeastward to the Moravian settlements at Wachovia, and then almost due south to the South Carolina town of Pine Tree Hill (Camden).[6]

The Great Wagon Road traversed the Catawba River Valley from north to south en route from Wachovia to Pine Tree Hill. The Catawba River, arising in North Carolina and continuing into South Carolina, was a slow-moving, muddy river. Its valley was broad and fertile. Because of its lushness and accessibility, it was the site of some of the first backcountry settlements in South Carolina. The Waxhaws, one of the larger backcountry settlements, was situated in the Catawba River Valley. In 1769 John Stuart, who was royal superintendent of Indian affairs for the Southern District, wrote that "near the Boundary, that Country is full of inhabitants, which in my memory was considered by the Indians as their hunting Ground, such is their rage for settling far back."[7]

What was it that caused this veritable flood of new settlers into the South Carolina backcountry? Cheap and available land was the primary attraction. South Carolina had a more generous land policy for settlers than did either Virginia or North Carolina. Each male head of household could claim one hundred acres for himself and an additional fifty acres for each member of his family and each servant. All that was required was that the settler enter a memorial at the land office in Charleston (something that many settlers neglected to do). South Carolina also had a long-standing tradition of religious toleration. And for those who thought about growing crops for export, South Carolina had a major port. So, while some settlers from Pennsylvania stopped off in Virginia and North Carolina, other settlers from those colonies joined the migration southward.[8]

The initial group that headed south was made up almost entirely of Scots-Irish. These were ethnic lowland Scots who, because they were Protestant, had been encouraged by the English government to settle in northern Ireland. For years religious intolerance has been given as the reason for the Scots-Irish immigration. But the real reason was economics. In the early eighteenth century, absentee landlords began to raise rents and shorten leases. And in the 1770s, the linen industry was beset with difficulties. With very little hope of prospering in Ulster, the Scots-Irish immigrated to Pennsylvania. There, they ran afoul of the Quaker government, which had little concept of what was occurring on the Pennsylvania frontier. If there were problems, the Quakers in Philadelphia were sure that it was the settlers and not the Indians who were responsible.[9]

Having little patience with governments with which they disagreed, the Scots-Irish decided to leave. They were a determined bunch, characterized by one historian as "undisciplined, emotional, courageous, aggressive, [and] pugnacious." But, he allowed, "they nevertheless produced ambitious leaders with the virtues of the warrior and politician."[10]

Although most of the Scots-Irish came to South Carolina after living in Pennsylvania or Virginia for a while, a large number came directly from Ulster in 1772 at the urging of the Reverend William Martin. This exodus was occasioned by an incident involving one of Martin's parishioners, a man named Beck. When Mrs. Beck was in labor with their first child, the local landlord's rent collector appeared. He gave the Becks two choices: immediate payment of all money due or immediate eviction. In a rage, Beck literally tossed the collector out of the house and, in the tussle, broke the man's neck. Mrs. Beck and the child died, and Beck disappeared.[11]

In a blistering sermon to his Londonderry congregation, Martin warned them that this was their future in Ulster under British rule. On 3 January 1772, he posted a notice on his church door of a "favourable opportunity" to go to South Carolina, where people could "enjoy life in abundance with the free exercise of their religious sentiments." In September 1772, some 467 families heeded the clergyman's call and left Ulster for South Carolina. They landed in Charleston and made their way by foot to the Catawba River Valley.[12]

The Scots-Irish were proud of their heritage. They were, first of all, Scots. They knew their nation's tortured history and its mistreatment by the English. They were fervent Presbyterians whose forebears had been persecuted for their beliefs. They were family men and women and tended to stick close by their kinfolks. They frequently emigrated in groups—either as families or as friends and neighbors with relationships reaching back to Ulster. Within the space of a generation, the upcountry was populated with families bearing such names as Adair, Bratton, Buchanan, Caldwell, Calhoun, Carroll, Collins, Davie, Jackson, Kuykendal, Lacey, Logan, Martin, McClure, Montgomery, Moore, Richardson, Ross, and Wardlaw.[13]

Two of what would become South Carolina's most famous families—the Jacksons and the Calhouns—were part of this eighteenth-century mass migration into South Carolina. In the 1760s, Andrew and Elizabeth Hutchinson Jackson, the parents of the seventh president, left County Antrim, Ireland, for Pennsylvania. However, they did not settle there. Almost immediately, they followed the lead of Elizabeth's sisters and hundreds of other Scots-Irish heading southward to the Carolinas, where they hoped they could make a better life for themselves. The Jacksons settled on

Twelve Mile Creek in the Waxhaws, and Andrew was born there. In the 1730s, the Calhouns left County Donegal, Ireland, for Pennsylvania. Later they moved to Augusta County, Virginia, where the family prospered. In 1756 Patrick Calhoun (the father of John C. Calhoun), his two brothers, and his widowed mother, Catherine, left Virginia for South Carolina. They established a new home first in the Waxhaws and then moved on to the Long Canes settlement along the Savannah River. Like the Waxhaws, Long Canes was a Scots-Irish stronghold.[14]

It is probable that the Calhouns, like most others moving down the Great Wagon Road, chose to do so after their fall crops had been harvested. If so, they would have traveled during the cold, rainy months from November to March. Sometimes in January and February snow and sleet made the trek even more uncomfortable. However, the immigrants endured the discomfort of winter travel so that they could be in their new homes in time for spring planting.[15]

Because travel was difficult, settlers were not able to carry much with them on their trek. Yet it was a rare family who did not take with them some special keepsake to use in their new home. When John Nuckolls left Virginia, he carried with him the cutting of a white rose, which he planted outside the door of his new cabin home. Ben Robertson's forebear, whom he called Great-great-great-great-great-aunt Narcissa, "packed the things she could not bear to leave—an *Arabian Nights* . . . , peach stones, hollyhock seed, seeds of melons and roses, knitting needles, a Bible." She also carefully wrapped a sugar bowl, "a piece of yellow crockery" that she had been given as a young bride in Pennsylvania and that had survived a number of moves on the frontier. Once her family reached the Valley of the Twelve Mile, she carefully planted her seeds.[16]

The rolling hills of the backcountry appealed to the new

arrivals. Early backcountry settlers took up whatever open lands they found so that they would not have to go to the trouble of clearing their fields. Those who settled on uncleared lands seldom took the time or expended the energy to chop down the large trees. Rather, they opted for *girdling*—cutting through the bark and cambium layer to the wood all around the trees—which caused them to die. It was a quick, easy method of getting enough land to plant new crops. Once their fields were established, they planted grain and Irish potatoes and raised livestock.[17]

Housing was also a concern for the new arrivals. Lean-tos made of pine branches were one quick fix. So was something called a "potato house," which was similar to a lean-to except that the frame was covered with sod rather than pine branches. These earthen-covered huts offered little protection from the elements, particularly during a hard rain. When time permitted, settlers cut down the massive pines for log cabins.[18]

Many of the settlers were poor, and their homes reflected their lack of worldly goods. "The People," wrote the Reverend Woodmason, "all new Settlers, extremely poor—Live in Logg Cabbins like Hogs—and their Living and Behavior as rude or more so than the savages."[19]

Typically these early cabins had but a single room and a dirt floor. Some had only three walls, but most had four. Roofs were made of bark or split logs. Sometimes clay was used for chinking in between the logs. The cabins seldom had windows. Any opening other than a door was small, with solid wooden shutters. Chimneys were made of local fieldstone or sticks and clay.[20]

Food and clothing were just as basic as housing. Corn was the first crop planted. Hogs were allowed to roam free in the forest until autumn, when they were rounded up for butchering. Generally there were just two meals a day, and the principal foods were cornbread and fresh pork in the winter and cornbread and bacon in the summer. There was some variety to this monotonous (and not very nutritious) diet. Vegetable gardens supplied turnips, pumpkins, and sweet potatoes. Native greens, such as poke, and berries and nuts could be found in the wild. Cows and chickens provided milk, eggs, and meat. In the Waxhaws, the Reverend Woodmason complained, all there was to eat was cornmeal, bacon, and eggs. "These people," he wrote, "are all from Ireland, and live wholly on Butter, Milk, Clabber and what in England is given to the Hogs and Dogs." In another location, he complained that he had had to subsist for weeks on "Musk Mellons, Cucumbers, Green Apples and Peaches and such Trash." For a delicate Englishman such as Woodmason—who missed his tea, roast beef, and pudding—backcountry cooking was "exceeding filthy, and most execrable." Perhaps if the good reverend had consumed a liquid other than water he might have had an easier time digesting backcountry fare. However, nowhere in his journal does he mention drinking corn whiskey, which was plentiful.[21]

Whatever was set on the table was eaten out of wooden trenchers or bowls. Gourds and wooden noggins were used for drinking and eating utensils; plates, glasses, and cups were scarce. If available, pewter spoons and hunting knives made eating easier, but there were no forks.[22]

Clothing, like everything else in the backcountry, was limited to not much more than the bare necessities. Women wore a simple shift, a short petticoat, and little else. Those who had good figures pinned their shifts "to shew the roundness of their Breasts, and slender Waists (for they are generally finely shaped)." Others pulled "their Petticoat close to their Hips to shew the fineness of their Limbs." Much of what we know about backcountry dress comes from Woodmason. Apparently the missionary spent some time ogling the women—before he wrote in disgust that they "might as well be in Puri Naturalibus—Indeed Nakedness is not censurable or indecent here, and they expose themselves quite Naked, without ceremony—Rubbing themselves and their Hair with Bears Oil." Men wore shirts and breeches, and children ran around "half naked." Everyone's clothing was roughly made, usually from linsey-woolsey or deerskins. Few settlers could afford shoes, and most went barefoot all year.[23]

It would not be unfair to say that the backcountry was close to being a state of nature. There were settlements, but the only social organization was the church. Woodmason was an Anglican missionary to the backcountry settlements, but there were only two Anglican congregations beyond Parish End. There were several Quaker meetings, but of those backcountry folk who belonged to a church (and fewer than 10 percent did), most were either Baptist or Presbyterian.[24]

Sectarian animosities were fierce. Scots-Irish Presbyterians were fervently devoted to their churches and just as fervently antagonistic to those who did not share their particular beliefs. They were the bane of Woodmason's existence and harassed him and any who attended his services. In one location, "[a] Presbyterian fellow carried off the Key to the Meeting House" so that services could not be held indoors. At Hanging Rock Creek, Woodmason was roughed up by "lawless Ruffians" who had been hired by "debauch'd licentious fellows, and Scots Presbyterians." When the missionary persisted in holding a service, "a Gang of Presbyterians" interrupted it by "hallooing and whooping . . . like Indians." In the High Hills of the Santee, some Presbyterians "hir'd a Band of Rude fellows to come to Service who brought with them 57 Dogs (for I counted them) which in Time of Service they set to fighting, and I was obliged to stop." A little later, Woodmason took a dog to the home of one of the area's leaders and informed him that "57 Presbyterians came that Day to Service, and that I had converted one of them, and brought Him home." He was fortunate to have been able to live to tell such a story.[25]

Frontier denominationalists took their religion seriously. The Baptists disliked Woodmason and his Anglican Church and did their best to discredit his missionary efforts. However, they liked the Presbyterians even less—and the Presbyterians returned the animosity. So deeply held were these feelings that "a Presbyterian would sooner marry ten of his Children to Members of the Church of England than one to a Baptist." There were more Baptists than Presbyterians in the backcountry, and although there were members of all churches in the various settlements, certain areas were the strongholds of one denomination or the other. The settlers in the Catawba and Savannah River Valleys were predominantly Presbyterian, while those living between the Broad and Saluda Rivers were mainly Baptists.[26]

Throughout the entire backcountry, there were twenty-one Presbyterian churches, but only two clergy. Several of these churches were very large—such as the Long Canes Church, which had five hundred families and was arguably the largest congregation in the colony. Baptist congregations did not require seminary-educated clergymen and allowed anyone to preach who had been called by the Holy Spirit. Before the Revolution, there were twenty-four organized Baptist churches and forty-nine Baptist meetinghouses in the backcountry. As important as organized religion was to individual communities such as the Waxhaws and Long Canes, 90 percent of the backcountry population was unchurched.[27]

The oldest and most important Baptist church was located on Dining Creek in the Fairforest community. The Reverend Philip Mulkey moved there in 1762, and the faithful erected a log meetinghouse. A decade later, the congregation of three hundred families was prosperous enough to afford a house of worship. They built a brick church that was forty by twenty-six feet and included galleries. The Fairforest Church established at least nine branch congregations in other frontier communities before the Revolution.[28]

The relative unimportance of organized religion to the overwhelming majority of backcountry residents added to the social instability of the region. Non-churchgoers openly profaned the Lord's Day by hunting, fishing, drinking, playing cards, and frolicking. Because of sectarian feelings, little respect was paid by church members to any beliefs but their own.[29]

This lack of community respect carried over to magistrates' courts. Justices of the peace had very little authority to begin with, but what little they had was eroded by the way many conducted their proceedings. Frequently taverns were the only sizable structure in an area, so the magistrates opted to hold their courts in them. Court Days were occasions more for entertainment than for the dispensing of justice, and local drunks took great delight in hurling insults at the justices and the court proceedings.[30]

By the 1750s, backcountry society was still not very community-minded. Sectarian and ethnic animosities, individualism, and a general lack of respect for social and civic institutions resulted in a society that was disorganized and unstable. The Cherokee War (1760–61) would be the match that ignited this volatile mix. The result was a society that could best be described as dysfunctional.[31]

The sudden influx of thousands of settlers through the colony's back door, not through Charleston, disrupted the orderly plan of frontier settlement that the colony's government had initiated in 1730. Instead of settling into organized townships that were designed to ring Charleston with a series of fortified settlements, the new upcountry residents settled down wherever they chose. They were usually careful to apply for official land grants, but they sometimes selected lands that were claimed by the two major Indian nations of the interior, the Cherokee and the Catawba. The proximity of the new settlements to the Cherokee and the Catawba would eventually cause difficulties.[32]

In 1760 the Cherokee, angry at broken English promises and urged on by the French on the Gulf Coast, decided to attack South Carolina's frontier settlements. There had been rumors all along the frontier, and in late January some 250 settlers from Long Canes decided it would be best to move closer to the coast. Unfortunately, their wagons got mired in a bog, and while they were trying to get them out, a Cherokee raiding party attacked. The result was the death or capture of nearly forty women and children (including Catherine Calhoun). The dead were mutilated beyond recognition—a fate that befell another group of settlers several days later. Most of the adults were killed, but nine children survived, despite having been scalped.[33]

The Cherokee roamed at will almost to the lowcountry. The Long Canes settlements and those along the Tyger and Enoree Rivers were closer to Cherokee territory and were therefore in the greatest danger. The Waxhaws, because of its proximity to the Catawba (who remained firm allies of the English), came through the Cherokee War relatively unscathed. However, there was no safety in the upcountry. One settler said that "if I was to give one hundred Guineas to a person to Cross the Country . . . I could not get any person to Undertake it."[34]

Cruelty and brutality were the order of the day on both sides. A group of Cherokee voluntarily held hostage at Fort Prince George were murdered by their captors. When the English garrison at Fort Loudon surrendered under a flag of truce, they were mowed down by a hail of arrows and shot as soon as they left the safety of the fort. Responding to this crisis, the colonial Com-

mons House of Assembly in Charleston appealed to the government in London for assistance and raised the bounty on Cherokee scalps from 25 to 35 colonial pounds ($473 to $662 in 1996
dollars).[35]

Everywhere there was chaos. Desperate settlers abandoned
their homesteads and crowded into makeshift forts, where disease
and corruption took their toll. Those who remained outside the
forts helped themselves to everything that had been left behind.
Even members of the militia had sticky fingers. This taking of
others' property would continue long after the Cherokee were
subdued in 1761. The war unleashed numerous horrors on the residents of the frontier, but the complete breakdown of law and
order was the most demoralizing.[36]

The Treaty of Augusta in 1763 established a reservation for the
Catawba and pushed the Cherokee farther westward. Residents of
the Waxhaws would no longer have to worry much about the danger of an Indian attack. However, they would have to worry about
attacks by outlaw bands.

The war completely disrupted whatever organized society had
existed on the frontier. The continued influx of new settlers,
especially those bent on making trouble, did little to stabilize the
situation. Law-abiding folks called these less-than-desirable newcomers "low people," "riff-raff," or "Virginia crackers." They
were "hunters and squatters, absconded debtors, idlers, gamblers,
and unsavory refugees from the northern colonies, settlers who
had never recovered from the trauma of the Cherokee War,
deserters from the military forces, and, often, mulattoes, Negroes,
or people of mixed white, Indian, and Negro blood."[37]

By 1766 these undesirables had formed organized outlaw
gangs in South Carolina and were cooperating with other criminal
bands as far north as Pennsylvania. The Great Wagon Road
became their highway for crime. In the summer of 1766, a wave

of lawlessness engulfed the frontier settlements. No one was safe.[38]

John "Ready Money" Scott, a merchant in the Savannah River Valley, was attacked in his home. The gang members tied up Scott and applied a red-hot poker to parts of his body until he revealed where he had hidden his money. The militiamen in Camden were so fearful of retribution from the organized criminals in the area that they refused to muster and search for robbers known to be lurking nearby. In the Waxhaws, John Huggins saw four suspicious men approach his house. When he challenged them, two of them fled, but the other two assaulted him. In the ensuing scuffle, Huggins was shot through the neck.[39]

A few brave individuals managed to capture six outlaws. They were taken to Charleston for trial because there were no courts outside the colonial capital; nor were there any law enforcement officers. The lowcountry elite was oblivious to what was happening in the colony beyond Parish End.

It took a journey of two weeks from Long Canes to get to Charleston. Five of the six outlaws were convicted, but Lord Charles Greville Montagu, the newly arrived British governor, pardoned them. He wanted to begin his term by showing the people of South Carolina how merciful he and British justice were. The governor's pardon convinced backcountry leaders that if they wanted law and order, they would have to take matters into their own hands.[40]

During 1767, criminals operated with little fear of law enforcement. Law-abiding citizens were cowed into submission or coerced into cooperation. Outlaws expected storekeepers and tavern owners to become fences for their stolen goods and burned the businesses of those who refused. Some were killed. It took a while for the decent, law-abiding settlers to come up with a plan to restore law and order. Initially sectarian rivalries, personal feuds, and the natural personal independence of the Scots-Irish settlers hindered any attempt at concerted action.[41]

Then the tide turned. It was as if, collectively, the settlers realized that they had to act or their families and homes would be destroyed. They turned on the outlaws with a vengeance. Armed frontiersmen hunted down bandits and burned their hideouts. Those who were caught were whipped to within an inch of their lives. The outlaws gave measure for measure, however, and soon the backcountry was involved in open warfare between those who wanted to build communities and those who wanted to destroy them. Colonial officials were slow to react to the situation. When they did, they decided that the law-abiding-citizens-turned-vigilantes were the bad guys and the outlaws were the victims! In an action that underscored a complete lack of understanding of the problem, Governor Montagu ordered the vigilantes to disperse. His proclamation was ignored.

By the fall of 1767, the various vigilante groups scattered throughout the backcountry had begun to cooperate with one another. Soon they were calling themselves Regulators. The royal governor might have thought of the Regulators as "licentious spirits," but in fact they were the backcountry's leading citizens. Many of them were small planters who owned several hundred acres that they farmed with their families and perhaps a slave or two. Others were entrepreneurs who owned grist- and sawmills or operated country stores. They were men who had a stake in society and wanted not only to preserve it but to improve their holdings. In short, these were individuals who aspired to what we have long called "the American Dream."[42]

The Regulators were men who had worked hard for what they had and resented those who were lazy. They had carved their farms out of the wilderness, they had built mills, and they had established stores. They knew that if they failed to curb the lawlessness in the backcountry, they stood a good chance of losing everything for which they had labored so hard. Nowhere was this desire for law, order, and stability more evident than in the remonstrance (petition) that the Regulators sent to the colonial Commons House of Assembly.[43]

The lengthy preamble to the document (more than five thousand words) detailed the troubles facing backcountry residents.

> Our large Stocks of Cattel are either stollen or detroy'd. Our Cow Pens are broke up. . . . Houses have been burned. . . . Stores have been broken open and rifled. . . . Private Houses have been plunder'd; and the Inhabitants wantonly tortured. . . . Property is of no Value, except it be secure: How Ours is secured, appears from the foremention'd Circumstances, and from now being obliged to defend our Families, by *our own Strength: as Legal Methods* are beyond our Reach—or not as yet *extended* to Us.[44]

The preamble did more than catalog the sufferings of the law-abiding citizens of the backcountry. In insulting and sarcastic language, it condemned the negligence of the colonial government for permitting such a state of affairs to exist. Then followed a series of twenty-three requests, twelve of which dealt with courts and legal matters. The Regulators wanted law and order. They also wanted public schools, representation in the Commons House, churches (and clergy to staff them), and Bibles and prayerbooks for the poor. That was all well and good, but the remonstrance was an "in your face" document that offended the members of the Commons House of Assembly. Among the Regulators' requests was a law to set the fees of attorneys because those charged by Charleston lawyers were outrageous. According to item 16, South Carolina was "harder rode at present by Lawyers, than Spain and

Italy by Priests." The eighteenth request was to limit the number of lawyers in the assembly.[45]

The legislators (many of whom were lawyers) *were* offended and tabled the petition. Only after several Regulators apologized to the Commons House for the offensive language were the needs of the backcountry addressed. The legislators passed a circuit court act and created several new parishes in the backcountry. Of more immediate need, they authorized the creation of two ranger companies to bring the outlaws to heel. In effect, the colonial government deputized the Regulators.

Colonial rangers were mounted units that could move swiftly and effectively from one location to another. They had a mission, and they did what they were told to do—eliminate the bandits. They ignored colonial boundaries. From the Savannah River to Virginia, they tracked down outlaws. In North Carolina, they hanged sixteen. Numerous criminals and their associates were flogged. Captured gang members were sent to Charleston, where they were tried and convicted. The worst offenders were hanged, and the others branded. Within six months, the outlaw bands had been broken up, their leaders either dead or decamped to other colonies. The criminals who had terrorized the citizens of the Waxhaws, Long Canes, Camden, and other backcountry settlements were no longer a threat.[46]

The Regulators, however, were not content. There still were "Rogues, and other Idle, worthless, vagrant People" who might be threats to individual property and the community. They needed to be disciplined. Who better to do this than the Regulators?[47]

In June 1768, Regulators from various settlements gathered in congress at the Congarees. This was a familiar backcountry area—the site of a former Indian village and later a trading post at the mouth of Congaree Creek in Saxe Gotha District—almost in the center of the colony. There they passed the Plan of Regu-

lation by which they intended to control the lives of "the baser
sort of people." South Carolina had no vagrancy law, so there was
no legal way to handle "idle persons." Given the temper of the
backcountry, the Regulators once again decided to take matters
into their own hands. For three years, it was not the royal government in Charleston but the Regulators who were in control of
South Carolina from fifty miles inland to Cherokee territory. The
Plan of Regulation was the only law that they recognized.[48]

The Plan of Regulation went far beyond simply imposing law
and order. It included provisions for regulating almost every
aspect of individuals' lives. If a man did not support his family, he
was disciplined. So were immoral women, debtors, drunks, loafers,
vagrants, or anyone thought to have had an association with the
outlaws. Whipping was the favored form of punishment: "39
lashes well laid on." One thing could be said for the Regulators—
they were effective. "The Country was purged of all Villans,"
wrote an observer. "The Whores were whipped and drove off. The
Magistrates & Constabls associated with the Rogues, Silenc'd &
inhibited. Tranquility reigned. Industry was restor'd."[49]

With no one to oppose them, some Regulators used their
movement as a cover to settle old scores. Enforcement of the Plan
of Regulation became capricious and, increasingly, vindictive. Pun-
ishments were used not just to bring offenders into line but to
humiliate and intimidate. Jacob Summeral, a justice of the peace
in New Windsor Township, fell into disfavor and was dragged
from his house and whipped. He refused to give up his commission and was kidnapped and tied to a post for seven days. He was
freed only because his wife managed to elude the Regulators and
get help from royal authorities and sympathetic militia.[50]

Another, more brutal, incident also occurred in New Windsor
Township. John Harvey, a farmer, was accused of having a horse
that belonged to someone else. A group of fifty or so Regulators

seized him and carried him off to be disciplined. He was chained to a tree, and each man whipped him ten times with bundles of switches. Throughout the administration of more than five hundred lashes some Regulators provided background music with drums and fiddles. Harvey survived, but this and other sadistic actions led to a backlash against the Regulator Movement.[51]

Law and order had been one of the Regulators' main demands. However, when victims of their lynch-style justice went to Charleston to swear out warrants for assault, armed bands of Regulators prevented the colony's provost marshal from arresting the offenders. They ignored royal proclamations to disband and disperse. Thus, the proponents of law and order became lawbreakers.[52]

Victims, justices of the peace, and respectable landowners decided that enough was enough. The organization that had been created to bring about law and order had become a threat to the stability and harmony of the backcountry. A new organization, composed of men calling themselves the Moderators, took up arms themselves and began to arrest Regulators. After several years of undisputed sway over South Carolina's interior, the Regulators were not about to give up easily. It made little difference that many of the Moderators were ex-Regulators and their neighbors. The Regulators were determined to maintain control of the backcountry, and the only way to do so, they reasoned, was to eliminate the Moderators.

In March 1769, some six or seven hundred Regulators marched on a Moderator camp on the banks of the Saluda River. The two sides were about equal in numbers, and both were spoiling for a fight. Bloodshed was avoided because two of the backcountry's recognized leaders, Richard Richardson and William Thomson, arrived on the scene. They argued that there was no real need for the Regulators since the riff-raff had long since either been brought to heel or fled to more hospitable colonies. The colonial assembly had passed an act creating circuit courts for the back-country. And if there was no need for the Regulators, then there was no need for the Moderators either. Through force of personality, Richardson and Thomson convinced both sides to disperse and allow the law to "take its course without opposition."[53]

The military truce in the backcountry coincided with actions by the Commons House of Assembly in Charleston. The assembly passed a new circuit court act that created seven district courts—four of which were designed to serve the frontier portions of the colony. Within three years, courthouses and jails would be built in the backcountry villages of Ninety Six, Orangeburg, Cheraw, and Camden. Law and order, one of the principal demands of the Regulators, would soon be a reality.

In 1763 the Indian nations of the Southeast had all signed the Treaty of Augusta with Great Britain. With the ensuing imperial control of Indian relations and the careful delineation of Indian territory, there was little conflict between Native Americans and settlers in South Carolina. Moreover, the outlaws were subdued and the rival vigilante groups dispersed, leaving law-abiding settlers free to improve their economic condition. In the remaining years before the American Revolution, this is what they did. They paid little attention to the growing revolutionary movement in Charleston and, instead, concentrated on their farms, orchards, herds, mills, and stores.

Although the majority of backcountry residents were subsistence farmers, by the late 1760s a number were becoming substantial planters. Indigo, wheat, hemp, and tobacco were grown for export as well as domestic consumption. With nine to twelve hands growing indigo, a backcountry planter could earn an income of between $22,000 and $44,000 (in today's dollars). More successful planters, such as Patrick Calhoun, became slave owners.

According a contemporary account by Henry Laurens, many settlers lived "comfortably in respect to every article necessary for the support of life."[54]

Even subsistence farmers were accumulating property and possessions. William Purse lived in the area between the Broad and Saluda Rivers. When he died in 1772, he owned two horses, three head of cattle, several hogs, two plows, and carpenter's tools. Among his household effects were a spinning wheel, deerskins, pewter utensils, kitchen items, and a "homemade jacket."[55]

In addition to working the land, some backcountry settlers became entrepreneurs. Country stores appeared along roadsides, and water-powered mills at falls in creeks and rivers. It was not unusual for a miller to charge one-tenth of whatever he ground for his customers. Thus, if a farmer's corn produced ten bushels of cornmeal, the miller kept one of them. Cattle driving was another way for an enterprising man to make a living. In the fall of the year, cattlemen herded cattle from the surrounding area into "cow-pens" before driving them to market in Charleston or Philadelphia. Hogs were also rounded up and, in the fall, driven to Charleston. Individuals with wagons pulled by horses or oxen transported the produce of the backcountry to Charleston. By the 1770s, roads threaded the forests and linked frontier communities with the provincial capital.[56]

In 1762 William Hill, a native of northern Ireland, immigrated to South Carolina from York County, Pennsylvania. He settled in the section of the Catawba River Valley that was called New Acquisition District. There was iron ore on his property. The mineral deposits were near the surface, and in the 1770s Hill began operating an open-pit mine.[57]

Joseph Kershaw of Camden had trading connections with the largest Charleston mercantile firms. Within a few years, he had established a thriving trade and branched out into planting. By the

Revolution, he owned more than one thousand acres of land and one hundred slaves. His home, on a prominent rise outside town, was as elegant as any Charleston mansion. It made the social statement that its owner had arrived. Moses Kirkland settled on the Wateree River, where he operated a sawmill, a gristmill, and a ferry. In 1775 he sold his mills and moved further inland to Ninety Six District, where he established himself as a successful indigo planter.[58]

Not only were those who had been in South Carolina for a while beginning to prosper, but so were newcomers. John Thomas Sr. and his wife Jane Black Thomas emigrated from Pennsylvania to the Catawba River Valley. They cleared a farm along Fishing Creek and were members of the Fishing Creek Presbyterian Church. In the mid-1770s, the Thomases moved to the Fairforest community in Spartan District. They were founders of the Fairforest Presbyterian Church, and Jane was "one of its most active and zealous members." John Thomas, unlike the overwhelming majority of backcountry residents, had the means to acquire several slaves.[59]

In 1773, Anthony Hampton moved from Rowan County, North Carolina, to South Carolina. Hampton, then fifty-eight, was descended from an English family who had settled in Virginia in 1620. Seeking greater economic opportunity, Anthony had moved first to the settlement of Town Fork in the Dan River Valley of North Carolina. In addition to his farming activities, he processed flax and soon developed a steady trade with Charleston. In the late 1760s, his three oldest sons ventured southward and became successful deerskin traders. Like their father, they established commercial ties with Charleston merchants. Their wagons hauled deerskins to the coast and returned to the frontier with Indian trade goods.[60]

At the urging of his sons, Anthony Hampton and his wife,

Elizabeth Preston Hampton, agreed to move to Spartan District near the boundary with the Cherokee nation. The Hampton's new home on Hampton Branch between Middle and South Tyger Rivers was their fourth in thirty years. Anthony Hampton was not just another footloose frontiersman who skipped from place to place—usually one step ahead of the sheriff. He had been an active member of the several communities in which he had lived. In Virginia he had been a tax official and in North Carolina a captain of rangers, road commissioner, and member of the General Assembly. The Hamptons' decision to move once again could not have come easily. Their children were all adults, and they were established members of their community. Yet, in 1773, Anthony Hampton sold his plantation in North Carolina, packed up all his worldly possessions, and, with three generations of his kin, moved to the South Carolina backcountry.[61]

Two years later, in 1775, William Bratton and his family arrived in South Carolina. The Brattons, like so many others in the backcountry, traced their roots to Ireland. In the early 1740s, Andrew Bratton of County Antrim had immigrated to Pennsylvania. Two of his sons, William and James, moved on south to Augusta County, Virginia.[62]

William's son, William, left Virginia and settled in Rowan County, North Carolina. Like many Scots-Irish, he was restless until he had settled where he wanted to put down deep roots. The land in Rowan County was fine, but along the Great Wagon Road there were stories of the rich lands farther south. In 1765, while still living in North Carolina, he purchased two hundred acres of land near Fishing Creek in the Catawba River Valley in what was then the southern portion of Mecklenburg County, North Carolina. Three years later, he took out a land grant adjacent to his new holdings. In 1772 the colonies of North and South Carolina adjusted their common boundary, and Bratton's property ended up in New Acquisition District of South Carolina. The colonial boundary meant little, however, to the residents of the Catawba River Valley. The valley, not some artificial surveyor's line, was of more importance to them.[63]

In 1774 Bratton had his South Carolina land surveyed, and the next year he and his wife, Martha Robinson Bratton, moved. They were newcomers in an area that had been settled for a generation. Farmsteads dotted the countryside. White's Mill on Fishing Creek ground grain for the farms in the vicinity. Nearby was William Hill's iron mine. Roads linked the town of Yorkville with trading centers in North and South Carolina. Fishing Creek Presbyterian Church, the spiritual heart of this Scots-Irish community, was already twenty-two years old.[64]

In the 1770s, backcountry residents were preoccupied with improving the economic well-being of their families. The political squabbles between the elite-dominated Commons House of Assembly and royal officials had little relevance for them. After all, many of the same members of the assembly who were complaining of British tyranny had dismissed the petitions of the backcountry populace as unworthy of notice. The revolutionaries Christopher Gadsden and John Rutledge had been particularly obnoxious. In letters to the editor of the *South Carolina Gazette and Country Journal*, Gadsden made light of backcountry complaints as "artful Insinuations and mischievous Catches," and Rutledge sneeringly referred to the backcountry population as a "Pack of Beggars." Thus, while members of the lowcountry elite became more and more concerned about their "rights as Englishmen," their political concerns were not shared by those in the backcountry. Beyond Parish End, the issue in 1775 and 1776 was the economy, period.[65]

While former Regulators and former Moderators were equally concerned with improving farms, expanding trade, and developing industry, the backcountry population was united on little else. Sectarian and ethnic animosities still simmered. Victims of the Regulator Movement still harbored grudges. And old Regulators were concerned, not that the movement had gotten out of hand, but that it had not gone far enough.

In many ways the troubles of the 1760s were but a prelude to those that would occur during the Revolution. Despite its progress since 1770, backcountry society was still relatively fragile. The American Revolution, like the Cherokee War, would set in motion a chain of events that rent the social fabric of the backcountry. In the 1760s, the area had divided into armed camps, with neighbor pitted against neighbor in the struggle for control of the frontier settlements. During the Revolution, the divisions were sharper and the stakes much higher—the future not just of the backcountry but of South Carolina and the United States of America depended on the outcome.

2

In the Eye of the Storm:
The Revolution in South Carolina,
1775–1779

The Council of Safety . . . by these presents testify—that they have nominated appointed and commissioned the Hon. Wm. Drayton and the Rev. Wm. Tennent to go into the interior parts of this Colony at the public expense, there to explain to the people at large the nature of the unhappy public disputes between Great Britain and the American Colonies—to endeavor to settle all political disputes between the people—to quiet their minds, and to enforce the necessity of a general union to preserve themselves and their children.

· SOUTH CAROLINA COUNCIL OF SAFETY, 23 JULY 1775

B y 1770 the backcountry had quieted down. Although there were now a handful of backcountry representatives in the Commons House of Assembly, frontier residents paid little attention to what was going on in Charleston. They were more concerned about the price of wheat and tobacco and improving their farms than they were about politics. Yet during the next ten years, the consequences of the actions of lowcountry politicians would threaten their homesteads and their very lives.

In their opposition to British actions in the 1770s, many American colonists raised the cry of "no taxation without representation." In South Carolina, the members of the lowcountry elite were not too worried about paying a few pennies more for imported items. Local issues, especially those that might threaten their power, were more important. The Commons House of Assembly was the means by which they were able to exert considerable control over the governance of the colony. In 1770 and 1771, the assembly became embroiled in a dispute with imperial officials over how it could spend the tax money it raised in South Carolina. The British government insisted that the governor and the Royal Council had to agree to all expenditures and that the assembly could not appropriate money for any purpose outside South Carolina. It was a serious constitutional issue that threatened the hard-won prerogatives of the Commons House. Neither side would back down. As a result, in 1771 royal government ground to a halt. A royal governor and other officials in Charleston were still functioning, but the assembly—when called into session—refused to act. Most South Carolinians simply ignored the British establishment and went about creating an alternative government.[1]

In December 1773, Charleston's Sons of Liberty called a meeting to protest the arrival of East India Company tea. Those present at the meeting passed a resolution to refuse to purchase the tea and to encourage others to do the same. The tea was unloaded and stored in the basement of the Charleston Exchange until 1776, when it was sold to purchase weapons for the new state of South Carolina.

Although the tea protest got a lot of attention, the more important action taken at the December 1773 gathering was the formation of the General Committee, which laid the foundations for a

separate government in South Carolina. When word arrived in
Charleston of Parliament's passage of the Intolerable Acts as punishment for the Boston Tea Party, there was an organization in
place to take action.

The committee sent out an announcement that there would
be a General Meeting in Charleston on 6 July 1774 and that delegates from all sections of the colony should attend. This was the
first time that the backcountry—with a majority of the white population—would have something more than a token presence.
The meeting adopted resolutions protesting the Intolerable Acts.
The resolutions were not merely a gesture of intercolonial soli-
darity but an expression of genuine concern for the future of liberty in the British colonies. For if Parliament could alter the
Massachusetts government and close the port of Boston, it could
do the same to South Carolina and Charleston. After the speeches
and resolutions, delegates were elected to the First Continental
Congress.

The representatives at the General Meeting also created the
Committee of Ninety-nine to act in its behalf. This group, com-
prising fifteen artisans, fifteen merchants, and sixty-nine planters,
became the de facto government of South Carolina. Much to the
consternation of imperial officials, the Commons House met and
appropriated funds to underwrite the cost of sending South Carolina's delegates to the Continental Congress.

Within six months, the Committee of Ninety-nine had
announced and held elections for South Carolina's First Provincial
Congress—another step on the road to creating an independent
government. The apportionment of the seats in the Provincial
Congress was a clear indication that while the lowcountry elite
wanted the backcountry with it in opposing the British, it had no
intentions of sharing its power with frontier residents. The backcountry, with 60 percent of the white population, was given only

55 seats out of 187. Sixty percent of the voters were allotted just 30 percent of the seats. The members of the lowcountry elite were behaving toward the backcountry population with an imperiousness not unlike the manner in which British officialdom treated them.

During the first six months of 1775, the Provincial Congress selected a Council of Safety to oversee the defense of the colony from attack by British forces. It organized successful raids on the royal powder magazines outside Charleston, seizing about sixteen hundred pounds of powder. Under the cover of darkness, a daring group of patriots entered the armory in the basement of the statehouse in downtown Charleston and made off with eight hundred muskets and two hundred cutlasses. And the Provincial Congress raised and equipped three new militia regiments.[2]

From outward appearances, South Carolinians seemed to be united in their defiance of the British Empire. That, however, was far from the case. In Charleston, vocal opponents of the Provincial Congress were silenced by physical threats or banishment to the countryside. The overwhelming black majority in the lowcountry was a matter of grave concern. As an example of what would happen to any black Carolinian who aided the British, Thomas Jeremiah, a free person of color, was hanged for saying he would help his king's forces if they came to South Carolina.[3]

Dealing with the backcountry was a bit more problematic. For nearly a generation, residents of the interior portions of the colony had been slighted by the lowcountry-dominated Commons House of Assembly. At best, backcountry folk were treated as second-class citizens; at worst, they were simply the first line of defense against the Indians. The malapportionment of the Provincial Congress reflected the power of the lowcountry elite and the disdain with which it regarded its country cousins.

Therefore, it is no wonder that reports began filtering down to

Charleston about open opposition to the Provincial Congress. One of the most outspoken critics was Thomas Fletchell, a well-known backcountry planter who lived in the Fairforest community between the Broad and Saluda Rivers. In a letter to Henry Laurens, the president of the Council of Safety, Fletchell declared: "I am resolved, and do utterly refuse to take up arms against my king, until I find it my duty to do otherwise and [am] fully convinced thereof." Fletchell was not alone. The Reverend Philip Mulkey, the pastor of the Fairforest Baptist Church, counseled his flock to remain loyal to the Crown. There were a number of others in the backcountry who considered the confrontation with Great Britain a lowcountry problem. That was a message that Lord William Campbell, the last royal governor, encouraged in his communication with backcountry loyalists.[4]

The South Carolina backcountry was seriously divided over what to do in 1775. Ethnic origin or religious beliefs provided no simple explanation of why individuals became patriots or Tories. A number of Scots-Irish newcomers became loyalists because they were afraid that they might lose their government land grants. However, in the Waxhaws the population was "universally [Scots-] Irish and universally disaffected." The English and Scots-Irish in the territory between the Broad and Saluda Rivers were evenly split, while the Germans in Saxe Gotha District were almost all Tories. The Quakers in the Bush River Valley were pacifists, but their co-religionists in the Camden area supported the king. When forced to make a choice, backcountry folk did, albeit reluctantly in many cases. If they had had their druthers, they would just like to have been left alone.[5]

Without the support of the backcountry, the revolutionaries would be in difficult straits. They realized that they needed to attract the support of community leaders, men of property who had risen to prominence during the Regulator Movement.

William Hill, Richard Richardson, William Thomson, and Joseph Kershaw had already cast their lots with the Revolution, but others, such as Robert Cunningham and Thomas Fletchell, remained loyal to the Crown.[6]

In an attempt to "fully convince" Cunningham, Fletchell, and other backcountry leaders of the justice of the patriot cause, the Provincial Congress sent a delegation to the interior. It consisted of five individuals: Oliver Hart, a Baptist clergyman; William Tennent, a Presbyterian minister; William Henry Drayton, a member of the Council of Safety; and two of the most prominent individuals in the backcountry, Joseph Kershaw of Camden and Richard Richardson of the High Hills.[7]

The delegation was "politically correct" fully two centuries before the term came into being. Drayton represented the Provincial Congress and the lowcountry elite, but his haughty presence was tempered by the inclusion of the two clergymen whose denominations were the ones most commonly found in the backcountry. The addition of Kershaw and Richardson gave evidence that the lowcountry elite dealt on equal terms with at least some men in the backcountry.

The response to the delegation was muted and mixed. Tennent wrote that many in the backcountry believed "that no man from Charleston can speak the truth and that all the papers are full of lies." Several crowds were small and openly hostile. For example, at King's Creek, Drayton and company had to listen to Thomas "Burnfoot" Brown denounce the patriots as savages. Just two weeks earlier, when he had declined to sign a revolutionary petition, a mob struck him down, scalped him, and then tarred his legs and held them over a fire. He lost two toes in the incident and became an implacable foe of the Revolution.[8]

As the patriot delegation warmed to its task, it began to have greater success. On 11 August 1775, at Jackson's Creek Meeting

House, the Reverend Tennent preached to a "pretty large congregation." After the sermon, he "harrangued the people an hour on
the state of the country." The congregation was "obstinently fixed
against the proceedings of the Colony," but eventually Tennent's
argument carried the day. He won over the leading men of the
area and persuaded an entire militia company to support the Revolution. Hart, preaching from the pulpit of the Fairforest Baptist
Church, did not have as much success.[9]

Drayton reported that many other settlers, especially the Germans, were "not with us." However, he should have noted that most
simply wished to be left alone. When words did not persuade the
populace, the delegation threatened force. It was not a tactic that
won many converts, but it did result in a document called the
"Treaty of Ninety Six." Some leading Tories refused to go along,
but a large number seemed willing to accept neutrality. Under the
terms of this agreement, backcountry opponents of the Provincial
Congress agreed not to render military aid to any British forces
that might enter South Carolina. In return, they received a vague
promise that they would be left alone.[10]

And backcountry Tories were very much alone. Shortly after
the signing of the "treaty," Governor Campbell fled Charleston for
the safety of a British warship in the harbor. Although he had been
in regular communication with the king's friends in the interior—
several of whom risked their necks to meet with him—Campbell
evidently gave no thought to traveling inland to rally those loyal to
George III.[11]

The treaty was not worth the paper on which it was printed. In
a calculated move to smoke out the enemies of the Revolution,
Drayton taunted Robert Cunningham and several leading Tories.
When they responded, the Council of Safety ordered them
arrested and hauled off in chains to Charleston. This breaking of
the treaty led to a Tory uprising in October 1775.[12]

The fighting began when a Tory band commanded by Robert Cunningham's brother Patrick captured a patriot supply train with one thousand pounds of powder and two thousand pounds of lead. The Provincial Congress ordered Major Andrew Williamson and five hundred militia to retrieve the much-needed war matériel. Facing a superior force of fifteen hundred Tories, Williamson decided instead to build a fort at Ninety Six. On 19 November 1775, the Tories attacked Williamson's position, and the first blood of the Revolution in South Carolina was shed.[13]

The authorities in Charleston were enraged. Neutrality would no longer be an option. The men of the backcountry would have to make up their minds and choose to support the Revolution . . . or else. There was no room in South Carolina for anyone who thought otherwise. Once again, the Council of Safety turned to one of the backcountry's acknowledged leaders, Colonel Richard Richardson of the High Hills. He issued a proclamation calling upon the residents of Ninety Six District to surrender the perpetrators, who were "robbers, murderers, and disturbers of peace and good order," and to return the powder and lead. Then, with a force of three thousand men, he marched toward Ninety Six. By mid-December, he had captured a number of eminent Tories (including Thomas Fletchell, who was found hiding in the hollow of a large sycamore tree) and the size of his army had nearly doubled to five thousand. On 22 December 1775, a detachment of Richardson's army surprised the Tories in their camp. The so-called Snow Campaign was a rout. As thirty inches of snow fell, the defeated loyalists were rounded up and forced to sign a document pledging not to take up arms again—on pain of losing all their property.[14]

With momentary peace in the backcountry, the Provincial Congress concerned itself with taking another step, albeit a halting one, toward independence. On 26 March 1776, South Carolina

became the second of the thirteen colonies to adopt a state constitution. (New Hampshire was the first.) The document began with
a lengthy listing of the abuses of George III, Parliament, and
imperial officials (including Governor Campbell, who was accused
of using "his utmost Efforts to destroy the lives, liberties and
properties of the good people here"). Because of the "present situation in American affairs," it was "indispensably necessary" that
South Carolina establish a government "by common consent, and
for the good of the people." Belying the bitterness of the recent
fighting in the backcountry, the constitution would be in effect
only "until an accommodation of the unhappy differences
between Great Britain and America can be obtained (an event
which, though traduced and treated as rebels, we earnestly
desire)." Drafted by a committee of the Provincial Congress, it
was adopted by that body without any consultation with the people. Noticeable to those who read it was the continued malapportionment of the General Assembly in favor of the lowcountry
districts.[15]

While not eliminating the possibility of a rapprochement with
the Mother Country, the General Assembly also continued its
preparations for the defense of South Carolina against the possibility of a British invasion. In March, Colonel William Moultrie
was ordered to Sullivan's Island at the entrance to Charleston Harbor to command an as-yet-unfinished palmetto-log-and-sand fort.
Gun emplacements were constructed along the city's waterfront.
Warehouses and stores on the wharves along East Bay Street were
leveled to give the batteries unobstructed fields of fire at any
approaching enemy warship.

On 1 June, a British fleet arrived at the entrance to Charleston
Harbor. Strong winds kept the ships outside the harbor for three
weeks—more than enough time for reinforcements to arrive in
Charleston. The fort on Sullivan's Island, however, was still

incomplete when the battle began on the twenty-eighth. Nothing went right for the British, and everything went well for the South Carolinians.

General Sir Henry Clinton landed his troops on Long Island with a plan that they would wade across Breech Inlet to Sullivan's Island and invade the fort from the rear. There was, however, a small problem. Clinton's intelligence was faulty. At low tide, the inlet was more than six feet deep, with a strong undertow and riptides. After assembling a small fleet of landing craft, his amphibious invasion was driven off by backcountry sharpshooters firing from behind a palmetto-log-and-sand breastwork.

The ships of the royal navy anchored off the island and began firing broadside after broadside at the fort. Some guns overshot their target. Those with better aim inflicted little damage: the cannonballs either buried themselves in the sand or bounced off the spongy palmetto logs. At the height of the battle, the South Carolina flag (indigo blue with a silver crescent in the upper left-hand corner) was shot from its staff. Ignoring the danger, Sergeant William Jasper, a recent volunteer, leaped upon the ramparts, picked up the flag, and tied it to a gun plunger. Jasper's heroism heartened his comrades, who were enduring a blazing summer sun as well as the unceasing British bombardment.[16]

The guns of the fort kept up a slow, steady rate of fire and inflicted considerable damage on the warships and their crews. After dark, the British ceased firing and disengaged. They lost one ship, and another was severely damaged. Their casualties (115 killed, 64 wounded) were nearly five times those of the Americans (17 killed, 20 wounded). Among those wounded was Governor Campbell, who had urged the British to attack South Carolina's capital city. "Charles Town," he wrote the Earl of Dartmouth, "is the fountainhead from which all the violence flows. Stop that and the rebellion in this part of the continent will, I trust, soon be at an end." In this judgment, as in most others, Campbell was wrong. Charleston might have been the fountainhead of the Revolution, but it was not the source of violence in South Carolina. There was violence everywhere, especially on the frontier.[17]

In July 1776, the Cherokee launched a long-dreaded attack on the entire southern frontier, from Georgia to Virginia. The South Carolina settlements caught the brunt of the first raids. Among the victims were Anthony and Elizabeth Hampton and their son, Preston, who were cut down in the front yard of their home on Hampton Creek in Spartan District. In the Valley of the Twelve Mile, Narcissa Robertson was bludgeoned to death and scalped as she went to a spring near her cabin.[18]

The initial success of the Indian raiding parties caused panic throughout the frontier districts. However, the military organization created by the Council of Safety worked as well in the backcountry as in Charleston. The militia responded and went on the counterattack. Among the prisoners captured were Tories disguised as Indians. To backcountry patriots, this was proof positive that royal officials had incited the Cherokee to strike the colonists while they were preoccupied with the British along the coast. In history and fiction, this has been one of the more enduring myths of the Revolution in South Carolina. It was not true, but the charge was damaging to the loyalist cause and tremendous propaganda for the revolutionaries.[19]

Backcountry settlers of all political persuasions rallied and, in a ninety-day campaign under the leadership of Major Andrew Williamson, routed the Indians. From Charleston, William Henry Drayton urged Williamson to "cut up every Indian cornfield . . . and burn every Indian town." Williamson and his men needed little encouragement. In a savage campaign, the Cherokee towns in South Carolina were razed and their crops destroyed, orchards chopped down, and cattle killed. Any Cherokee unfortunate enough to be caught by the militia was either killed or sold into slavery. Once the Cherokee were the most feared Indian nation on the Carolina frontier, but after this defeat they were no longer a threat to white settlers. In May 1777, the Cherokee signed a treaty with South Carolina and abandoned their lands east of the Blue Ridge Mountains.[20]

With the departure of the Cherokee, there was no longer any serious danger to moving into the isolated river valleys of the piedmont. The thirteen colonies might be at war with the Mother Country, but not in South Carolina. The thirty months following the defeat of the Cherokee in October 1776 brought an artificial peace to South Carolina. The lull in the fighting produced an economic boom in the state, from the mountains to the sea.[21]

Hundreds of new immigrants pushed into the piedmont in something of a land rush. Among them was John Nuckolls Sr., who left his farm in Dinwiddie County, Virginia, in 1776 and took up lands along Thicketty Creek in Spartan District. There he built his house on a rise overlooking rich bottomland. Zechariah Bullock, Nuckolls's brother-in-law, followed him to South Carolina. On the east side of the Pacolet River, about four or five miles upstream from Grindal Shoals, Bullock found a site for his new farm. Thomas McCalla and his wife, Sarah, moved to South Carolina in 1778. Two years later, Charles Sims, a native of Hanover County, claimed land at the mouth of Tinker Creek on the Tyger River.[22]

The influx of new settlers was reflected in the composition of the delegations that the backcountry districts elected to the General Assembly. In the Third General Assembly (1779–81), of the eleven men elected for New Acquisition District the date of arrival in South Carolina is known for six. Three had moved to the colony in the mid-1760s, one in 1770, and two in 1778—just a year before their election. Three of the four representatives from Spartan District arrived in the 1770s; the fourth had come a few years earlier, in 1768. The Hampton family moved to South Carolina in 1773; in 1779, four of Anthony Hampton's surviving sons—Henry, John, Richard, and Wade—won seats in three different districts.[23]

The newness of the delegations reflected the newness of the settlements. There might be a war going on elsewhere, but not on the South Carolina frontier in the late 1770s. Men sought their opportunities where they could.

James Williams was a native of New Hanover County, Virginia. After his father's death, he moved to North Carolina, where his older brother and several cousins lived. In 1772, he settled along the Little River in Ninety Six District. Three years later, his neighbors elected him to the First Provincial Congress. Williams served in the Snow Campaign and in the 1776 campaign against the Cherokee. From 1776 until 1778, he devoted himself to improving his farm. Like many others on the frontier, he was something of an entrepreneur. He operated a flour mill and had plans for a sawmill. He was a whiskey trader and may have had his own still. In June 1779, he wrote his son Daniel that he was pleased to hear that "business goes on well," but advised him to increase the price of whiskey. In January 1780, he had sufficient cash on hand from his various enterprises to advance the men of his regiment their pay.[24]

Like Williams, William Bratton was a relative newcomer to South Carolina. He built a home just as the threat of war began to loom over the backcountry. The site he chose was a high ridge between the Broad and Catawba River Valleys. There were two springs within easy walking distance of the new house, and the Lincoln Road ran right by the front door.[25]

The house itself was constructed of hewn logs cut on the place. Although a log cabin, the Bratton home was several notches above most frontier dwellings. For one thing, the massive oak and pine logs were shaped. For another, the structure was built on raised fieldstone piers and had a plank floor. There were only two rooms in the house—one on the main floor and a loft room above. A massive brick chimney occupied one wall of the house, and there were fireplaces on both floors. Three steps led to a door in the chimney wall that concealed a staircase to the windowless loft. Like most Scots-Irish cabins, the Brattons' had both front and back doors. It was the only house in the area with glazed windows. Most cabins had solid wooden shutters, but the Brattons' had several small windows (about twelve to sixteen inches on a side) filled with four small panes. It also was one of the few cabins with a front porch. A porch was a place for relaxation and ease—uncommon practices among the spartan Scots-Irish. Because of the unsettled conditions on the frontier, there were small openings or gun ports on three sides of the second story of the cabin. The scale and details of the house all indicate that William Bratton was a man of some means.[26]

Although there was little military activity in South Carolina after the defeat of the Cherokee, there were occasional reminders that a war was being fought elsewhere.

In 1775, the Provincial Congress offered a bounty of £1,000 South Carolina currency (about $12,500 in today's dollars) to anyone who established an iron furnace. Responding to that economic opportunity, William Hill built an ironworks on Allison Creek in the Catawba River Valley. Isaac Hayne, a lowcountry planter, was his partner, but Hill operated the furnace. They named their enterprise the Aera Furnace, and in it Hill produced pig iron as well as consumer goods. Farmers for some forty miles around purchased his farm implements, kitchen utensils, and household items. Cast-iron firebacks to reflect the heat of a fire were popular items. Reflecting the mood of his community, Hill designed one with the slogan "Liberty or Death."[27]

With the onset of hostilities in 1776, Hill converted his operations from domestic implements to cannonballs and weapons. Two loans from the state of South Carolina helped finance the conversion and expansion of his operations. By the late 1770s, his workforce included ninety slaves.[28]

The thirty months' lull in the fighting also created economic opportunities along the coast. Rice plantations produced large crops for European markets. After the royal navy sailed from South Carolina in August 1776, Charleston Harbor bustled with ships from France, the Netherlands, and New England. Because they were cut off from their traditional trading partners in Britain, merchants established new commercial relationships. Privateers, operating under letters of marque from the state government, raided the shipping lanes of the British Empire. The royal navy instituted a blockade of Charleston Harbor, but it was a bit leaky, and skilled captains were able to bring their ships safely into port. Taverns and bordellos along the bay flourished as merchant sea-men and sailors from several countries found Charleston a wel-come port for rest and recreation. Fortunes were made in shipping, blockade running, banking, and insurance.[29]

There was fighting in New York and Pennsylvania, but the absence of military activity in South Carolina created a surreal peace from the mountains to the sea. It was as if Carolinians were in the eye of a hurricane and did not realize that the backwall of the storm could do more damage than the initial surge.

The public apathy was unsettling. Not many citizens took the trouble to exercise their right to vote. In the fall of 1776, elections for the Second General Assembly (1776–78) were held within a short time after the arrival of the news of the signing of the Dec-laration of Independence. Despite this momentous news and the knowledge that the upcoming assembly would revise the state's 1776 constitution, the voter turnout was abysmal. President Rawlins Lowndes bemoaned the fact that some members of the

Second General Assembly received only two or three votes; in some districts the only ballot casts were by the local polling officials. In St. Paul's Parish, Isaac Hayne got four votes and won a seat in the assembly. In New Acquisition District, William Hill would later remember, there was no official balloting. Instead, a caucus of citizens gathered at his ironworks and generally agreed on their representatives.[30]

Thus, the important work of creating a permanent state constitution fell to men who could hardly claim to be representing the people. And on a number of occasions when the assembly met, there were not enough representatives present to make up a quorum and conduct business.[31]

The most contentious issue facing the assembly was the disestablishment of the Church of England. Since 1706, the church had received financial support from the colonial treasury; only its ministers could legally record vital statistics (births, marriages, and deaths). It was a matter that rankled non-Anglicans, especially the Baptists and Presbyterians of the backcountry districts. The Reverend William Tennent drafted a memorial to the General Assembly that called for the disestablishment of the Church of England. In New Acquisition District, William Hill enthusiastically circulated copies of Tennent's memorial and urged all his neighbors to sign it. Hundreds did so. In the assembly itself, he forcefully argued for his cause: "With the new constitution let the day of justice dawn upon every rank of men in this state. . . . Let it be a foundation article in your constitution 'That there shall be no establishment of one religious denomination of Christians in preference to another. . . . Yield to the mighty torrent of American freedom and glory.' " After several test votes, the assembly unanimously agreed to support Tennent's position.[32]

After the constitutional debate, the General Assembly enacted a law requiring former royal officials and others of dubious loyalty to swear an oath of allegiance to the independence of South Carolina. Any individual who refused was to be banished from the state. So great was the civic torpor that the law was ignored. The following year, the assembly passed a draconian measure requiring every free male inhabitant of the state to renounce support of the king and Parliament and to swear true allegiance to South Carolina. Anyone who refused or neglected to take the oath would be barred from voting or holding public office and forbidden to sue in the courts, own land, or practice his profession. If a man left the state to avoid taking the oath, he would be considered a traitor and executed if he returned to South Carolina. As the deadline approached for registering the oath, government officials discovered to their dismay that the overwhelming majority of the people simply could not be bothered. Except for a demonstration or two by Charleston's Sons of Liberty in support of the measure, it had few champions. The deadline for compliance was extended several times, but not even avowed patriots bothered to take the oath.[33]

Not only were men disinclined to take the mandatory oaths of fealty to the state, but it was difficult to get men to enlist for military service. Those who did generally signed up for terms of three or six months. After doing a stint, they went back home to their farms. Between 1775 and 1781, Alexander Peden of the New Acquisition served five separate tours of duty, ranging from two weeks to six months. Henry Rea enlisted in 1775 and served until the end of the Cherokee Campaign in 1776. He then mustered out and did not reenlist until 1780. Thomas Boggs of the District Between the Broad and Catawba Rivers also participated in the expedition against the Cherokee in 1776 and, then, like Rea, left the service until 1780.[34]

There were disciplinary problems with the men who did serve. Yeoman farmers might enlist for three-month tours. However, if a planting or harvest season occurred during their enlistment, it was not unusual for men to leave their units and return home. Discipline was a serious problem, and insubordination and desertion were all too common.[35]

In 1778 the General Assembly agreed that up to one-third of its forces could be slaves who would serve in support roles to build fortifications and to man boats. A signing bonus of one hundred acres in what had formerly been Cherokee territory was offered to any volunteer. (This bonus was in addition to the one hundred acres promised by the Continental Congress.) But not enough volunteers stepped forward, so military duty in the Continental forces became the punishment for vagrants, anyone who harbored deserters, and those who hunted deer at night with fire.[36]

The following year, the assembly offered a cash bonus and a state note bearing 10 percent interest. Yet nothing seemed to work. In addition to the carrot of cash and land, there was the stick of heavy fines for not responding to duty when called. Dedicated patriots such as General William Moultrie considered the law too severe and a threat to liberty. Yet the General Assembly—even with a British army based just across the Savannah River—voted to reduce the term of enlistments from three months to two months. In certain circumstances, a commander could detain soldiers for another ten days. Then, no matter what the military situation, he had to release them from duty. Men might be pulling militia duty, but their hearts were not yet enlisted in the cause of the Revolution.[37]

For Carolinians who were not sympathetic to the patriot cause, the implementation of the new constitution and the passage of the fealty oaths created problems. Under the 1776 constitution, there was still hope of reconciliation with Great Britain. Now, in 1778, those controlling South Carolina had opted for independence. There might not be any military action, but it was clear that the time was coming when Carolinians would have to make a choice: to side with George III or with South Carolina.

In the Lower District Between the Broad and Saluda Rivers, those loyal to the king voted with their feet. Under the various agreements that had been worked out in 1775, they had just wanted to be left alone to plow their fields and raise their families. They viewed the oath as the first step toward being compelled to take up arms against the British government. This they would not do. In the spring of 1778, a group of five hundred men traveled to the British province of East Florida and became the nucleus of the Regiment of South Carolina Royalists.[38]

In neighboring Little River District, some loyalists joined the Florida exodus, but more remained. And in an interesting turn of events in 1778, they elected known Tories to the General Assembly. Voters chose Robert Cunningham, whose arrest had triggered the uprising of 1775, for the South Carolina Senate and Jacob Bowman and Henry O'Neall, both participants in the uprising, for the South Carolina House of Representatives. Neither Cunningham nor Bowman ventured to Charleston to claim his seat, but O'Neall did and took the necessary oaths of allegiance. The election returns in Little River District and the Florida exiles were reminders that while the backcountry might appear to be calm and peaceful, there were still strong loyalist undercurrents in the territory beyond Parish End.[39]

For South Carolina's loyalists, the arrival of a British invasion force off the coast of Georgia in late 1778 was welcome news. On 29 December 1778, Savannah fell to the British, who then controlled all of Georgia within a short time. In many a patriot household the loss of Georgia was a call to arms. In New Acquisition District, David Sadler and John Adair enlisted in the militia, and across South Carolina so did hundreds of others.[40]

Within the space of less than six weeks, the British controlled

Georgia. The royal governor returned, and for the remainder of the war, Georgia was once again a royal colony. General Augustine Prevost, the commander of British forces in Georgia, decided to test the determination of South Carolinians. He sent a small force by ship to Port Royal Island, where the South Carolina militia under General William Moultrie and General Stephen Bull drove the British away.[41]

For the Americans it was a Pyrrhic victory. The militia force melted almost as rapidly as the Wicked Witch of the West in *The Wizard of Oz*. Men were more concerned about protecting their families than protecting South Carolina, especially when Prevost entered South Carolina in full force in late April.[42]

Moultrie and his command rapidly retreated toward Charleston, burning bridges and ferries along the way. Unfortunately for the Americans, the weather was unseasonably dry and the rivers were running low. The British were able to ford the numerous rivers and creeks with little difficulty. On 9 May, Moultrie entered Charleston without attempting to defend the last river crossing at Ashley River Ferry. The British were right behind. Charleston, located at the tip of a peninsula, was not a haven for the Americans. It was a trap.[43]

Residents began to construct fortifications on the land approach to the city. By 11 May, the British reached the hastily built earthenworks defending Charleston. Inside the city was chaos and uncertainty. General Moultrie was determined to defend the city at all costs, but his resolve was not matched by that of the state's officials. Governor John Rutledge ordered Moultrie to send a message to Prevost inquiring as to what terms he "would be disposed to grant" should a capitulation be sought. Because the British could successfully storm the town, Prevost had only one reply: surrender.

The governor and his council debated the matter for nearly a day. Feelings ran strong that South Carolina had been abandoned by the other states and the Continental Congress and that the state should try to cut the best deal possible. They proposed to General Prevost that he would be allowed to take possession of Charleston "provided the State and Harbour should be considered as neutral during the war." The future of South Carolina— whether it would be one of the United States or revert to a royal colony—would be put off until the treaty ending the war.[44]

The British commander was not prepared to negotiate over civilian matters and insisted on dealing only with the future of men in uniform. They and the civilian authorities were to become prisoners of war. That message put some backbone into the government, and Moultrie's insistence on defending the city won out. The approach of an American army under General Benjamin Lincoln caused Prevost to break off the discussion and begin a retreat to Georgia.[45]

On John's Island, Thomas Fenwicke, a local planter, visited a militia camp and ate dinner with the officers. Many of them were his neighbors, but he betrayed their position to a British and Tory force that surrounded them. Sensing that their position was hopeless, the Americans asked for quarter—and were granted it. However, no sooner had they surrendered their weapons than the British and Tories attacked them with bayonets. Almost the entire company was either killed or wounded.[46]

As the British marched south, they pillaged every farm and plantation on their way. Nearly four thousand slaves were either carried off or followed the British army. A number of homes were burned, and so was Sheldon Church, one of the most impressive Anglican churches in what had been British North America.[47]

The British invasion of 1779 was a near thing. Left to their own devices, South Carolinians were outmaneuvered, outmanned, and unsure of what to do. Some supported the British as they marched through the lowcountry, but others rallied to protect their state and the new nation. The phony war of the previous thirty months had lulled all too many into a false sense of security.

The conduct of Prevost's troops was a wake-up call and turned many a latent loyalist into an angry patriot. The betrayal of neighbors, the cold-blooded murder of unarmed prisoners, and the wanton destruction of property provided a bitter foretaste of the civil war that would soon engulf South Carolina.

3

The Storm Surge Hits:
The Revolution in South Carolina,
1779–1780

I may venture to assert, that there are few men in South Carolina who are not either our prisoners, or in arms with us.
SIR HENRY CLINTON, 4 JUNE 1780

B y August 1779, the southern part of the South Carolina coast knew that the war was quite real. The British had marched to the very gates of Charleston and then retreated to the safety and comfort of the coastal island town of Beaufort. There they established a fortified base while a small British flotilla patrolled nearby Port Royal Sound, the best natural harbor on the South Atlantic coast.[1]

General Prevost's foray into South Carolina ended in mid-September 1779 with the arrival of a large French fleet off the Georgia coast. The nine hundred British and Hessian troops ensconced at Beaufort were hurriedly recalled to Georgia to help defend Savannah. They arrived just in the nick of time as the garrison was considering surrendering to a joint Franco-American task force. With Prevost's reinforcements, the British successfully defended the city during a three-week siege. On 9 October 1779, a frontal assault on the fortified British position failed and cost the allies dearly. Not only did they miss an opportunity to recapture Savannah and Georgia, but they suffered heavy casualties. Among the more than twelve hundred allied soldiers killed were Sergeant William Jasper, the hero of the Battle of Sullivan's Island, and Count Casimir Pulaski, the Polish nobleman who had crossed the Atlantic to help the colonies win their freedom. Following the defeat at Savannah, French Admiral Charles d'Estaing ordered his fleet to return to France.[2]

As 1779 drew to a close, the British were planning a major southern campaign. Encouraged by their successes in Georgia and the reports of loyalists in the Carolinas, they envisioned a quick victory that would roll up the southern states one by one. South Carolina was the key to their strategy. "I had long determined," wrote Sir Henry Clinton, "on an expedition against Charleston, the capital of South Carolina."[3]

On the day after Christmas 1779, a British fleet sailed from New York with an army of eighty-five hundred. The passage was anything but smooth, and several vessels and their military cargo were lost. In January 1780, the fleet rendezvoused off the Georgia coast. While repairs were made, Sir Henry Clinton and Vice Admiral Marriot Arbuthnot carefully plotted their strategy. They would not make the mistakes that had doomed the 1776 assault on Charleston.[4]

On 11 February 1780, British forces landed on John's Island, south of Charleston. General Lincoln and his army withdrew into Charleston and prepared to defend the city. The British moved slowly and did not reach the city's outer fortifications until March.

In a display of contempt for the locals that would lead to their undoing, the British captured Thomas Farr, the speaker of the South Carolina House of Representatives, and forced him and his son to herd cattle in their supply train. All the while they mocked him.[5]

On 1 April, the British began to construct their siege works. On 9 April, a British fleet of fourteen warships slipped past the forts defending Charleston and sailed into the inner harbor. Now the city was vulnerable to cannon fire from both land and sea. In an attempt to hinder British gunners, citizens painted the steeple of St. Michael's black—only to discover later that they had made the steeple more, not less, visible! From afar, George Washington knew that the city was lost once the British ships were able to enter the inner harbor. Yet Lincoln and the civilian authorities insisted upon defending the South Carolina capital.[6]

The noose was tightening around the American garrison, but rather than save his army, General Benjamin Lincoln let local politicians browbeat him into remaining in the city. On 13 April, Governor John Rutledge and several members of his council escaped the beleaguered city. The General Assembly gave the governor extraordinary powers to "do all other matters and things which may be judged expedient and necessary to secure the liberty, safety and happiness of this State, except taking the life of a citizen without legal trial." For nearly two years, Rutledge was the only civilian government in South Carolina.[7]

Those state officials who remained were determined to resist to the last man, and when Lincoln made plans for evacuating his troops, they threatened to open the city's gates to the enemy. After 15 April, it was only a question of when Charleston would surrender, not if. The British lobbed heated cannonballs into the city, setting many buildings on fire. Exploding shells from both sides made a spectacular show, which General Moultrie likened to "meteors crossing each other, and bursting in air; it appeared as if the stars were tumbling down." The bombardment was incessant for nearly a month and stopped only when either Lincoln or Clinton proposed negotiating the possibility of surrender. The damage to the city was considerable. Among the casualties was a marble statue of the British statesman William Pitt, which lost an arm to a passing cannonball.[8]

With almost all of the American military forces in the state trapped in Charleston, the British operated with impunity in the countryside. At Monck's Corner, Lieutenant Colonel Banastre Tarleton's British Legion (a mixed cavalry and infantry unit of Pennsylvania Tories—in the eighteenth century cavalry and mounted infantry were often called dragoons) surprised a small American unit. The Americans were routed, and a French officer attached to them asked for quarter. Instead of honoring the courtesies of war, Tarleton's men "mangled him in the most shocking manner" with sabers. Clinton obviously received a different report of the battle. In his memoirs, he wrote: "The precipitation with which the enemy had fled and the swampiness of the ground . . . prevented the slaughter which might else have probably ensued, and facilitated the escape of the rest." At nearby Fairlawn Barony, the home of the Colleton family, Lady Jane Colleton and several other women were physically attacked by men of Tarleton's legion. Lady Jane, a prominent loyalist, was slashed with a sword as she successfully defended herself from the attack of a would-be rapist. Although several of the dragoons involved were disciplined, their commander was not. These incidents, like the ones a year earlier near Beaufort, were clear indications of the depths to which the conflict in South Carolina would sink in the months to come.[9]

On 12 May 1780, after a forty-two-day siege, Lincoln surrendered his army of approximately five thousand men. It was one of the greatest disasters in the annals of the U.S. Army. By refusing to stand up to civilian authorities, he placed the entire future of the United States in jeopardy. There was now no American army in the South to oppose Clinton. South Carolina, the key state in Clinton's grand southern strategy, lay open to the victorious British army.[10]

Throughout the empire, the fall of Charleston was greeted with enthusiasm. In occupied New York, the *Royal Gazette* gloated over "conquest and complete reduction . . . of that opulent, populous, and very important colony." Dubliners placed candles in their windows in a grand illumination, a traditional eighteenth-century method of observing important occasions. In London, the victory was marked by the celebratory firing of muskets and cannon.[11]

Clinton's strategy seemed to be sound. He had captured the city and the forces—the American army in the South—against which he had "long determined" to mount an expedition. No doubt he and his staff were optimistic about the number of loyalists in the state. One of them later told General William Moultrie, "Sir, you have made a gallant defense, but you had a great many rascals among you . . . who came out every night and gave us information on what was passing in the garrison."[12]

Clinton directed James Simpson, a Charleston loyalist, to determine the political leanings of South Carolinians—especially those in the backcountry. On 15 May, Simpson reported that there were "great Numbers, who continue attached to His Majestys Government, and who will Join to effect the Reestablishment of it," if—and this was a very big if—the British government provided them with support and protection. He then divided the populace into four categories. In the first group were the well-to-do who had seen the error of their ways and were happy to have South Carolina once more under royal authority. The second category contained those who had no strong political convictions for either side but had been hoodwinked by the revolutionaries; they were now disenchanted with the American cause and willing to support the king. The third group were dedicated rebels, but the turn of events had convinced them that the American cause was hopeless. The fourth group consisted of unrepentant and hostile rebels. Interestingly, Simpson's analysis of the third and fourth categories was based on secondhand information: "I have thought it proper," he wrote, "to avoid a Conversation or Intercourse with any of them." That was a serious mistake, but in mid-May, in the euphoria that surrounded the victors, it was not noticed.[13]

The garrisons at Ninety Six, Camden, Beaufort, and George-town surrendered. General Andrew Williamson presented his troops with the option of retreating to the mountains and continuing the struggle or surrendering. Despairing of the American cause, Williamson's men chose to surrender, accept parole, and return to their homes.[14]

The terms that backcountry militia accepted were identical to those offered the Charleston garrison. Clinton's terms were not what Lincoln had sought, but then he was in no position to protest. All civilian males and militiamen in the city were to be considered prisoners of war. They were then paroled and allowed to return to their homes in peace. The officers and men of the Continental army were imprisoned. Under the circumstances, these were fairly generous terms.[15]

In rapid succession the British occupied four vital towns in the area outside of Charleston: the courthouse and market towns of Camden, Cheraw, Georgetown, and Ninety Six. The reaction of Georgetown's residents was fairly typical. They thought the American cause was lost, and the community's leading citizens signed an address to the British commander of the occupying garrison. In it they stated that "the original cause of the disputes between Great Britain and her colonies" over taxation without representation had been resolved by one of Clinton's proclamations. They concluded: "We are therefore desirous of becoming British Subjects in which capacity we promise to behave ourselves with all becoming fidelity and loyalty."[16]

In New Acquisition District, Colonel William Bratton and Colonel Samuel Watson called for a meeting of their regiment at the Bullock's Creek Meeting House. It was a dispirited group that gathered there. Bratton and Watson did not encourage their soldiers to carry on the fight. Instead, they allowed that it appeared that any further opposition to the British would be futile, and they advised "each of them to do the best they could for themselves." It appeared to many that the revolutionary movement in South Carolina was finished.[17]

It is little wonder that Clinton could boast to Lord Germain, the American secretary in London, that "there are few men in South Carolina who are not our prisoners, or in arms with us." Yet within less than six weeks, the backcountry would be up in arms and the British would be fighting desperately to control what they had thought was a conquered province.[18]

What caused such a rapid turnaround? It was not one single incident, but a series of incredibly stupid blunders by the British that led to a remarkable reversal of events.

The first, and one of the most significant, was General Clinton's proclamation of 3 June 1780 in which he abrogated the terms of surrender. According to older historical accounts, the "Revolutionary party was . . . completely broken up." The American cause was in dire straits. Those who had been willing to fight had surrendered and taken parole. They had returned to their homes where, as parolees, they expected to remain as neutrals for the duration of the conflict.[19]

Instead of leaving well enough alone and permitting the parolees to remain neutral, Clinton was determined to force "every man to declare and evince his principles" so that the loyalists in South Carolina would have the "opportunity of detecting and chasing from among them" any dangerous neighbors who might be closet rebels. Parolees now had the choice of either taking an oath of allegiance to the king (which carried with it an acknowledgment that they would take up arms against their former comrades still in the field) or being treated as "rebels and enemies to their country." And they had only seventeen days to make up their minds. After 20 June, any parolees who had not taken the oath of allegiance would be considered enemies of the king.[20]

The proclamation was a monumental error. In his memoirs, Clinton admitted as much, but pointed out that he left the province less than a week after the proclamation. Therefore, the consequences of the proclamation were all Lord Cornwallis's fault because he had the authority to counteract it.[21]

For the backcountry, the proclamation was particularly ill timed. Men had given their word that they would go home and sit out the war. Now the British government, through Clinton, was arbitrarily forcing them to become either "loyal subjects or rebels." They learned of this latest British perfidy on the heels of one of the most infamous incidents of the American Revolution, the cold-blooded murder of unarmed Americans by Banastre Tarleton's British Legion.[22]

On 29 May 1780, a small detachment of Continental troops (mostly Virginians) under the command of Colonel Abraham Buford was north of the Santee River when Charleston fell. With him were Governor Rutledge and several other government officials. Lord Cornwallis, given the task of pacifying the country outside of Charleston, was determined to capture the governor and end any semblance of resistance. Buford's force already had more than a week's head start, so that catching them seemed improbable. If anyone could do the job, however, it was Tarleton and his legion. In the relentless heat and humidity of a South Carolina June, Tarleton cajoled his men into riding more than one hundred miles in a little more than two days. They came within a matter of hours of capturing Governor Rutledge.[23]

The governor was staying at Rugeley's Mill north of Camden. Warned of Tarleton's approach, he fled in the middle of the night. Several hours later, Tarleton's advance guard reached the mill. Buford's force was about twenty miles away in the Waxhaws settlement. Tarleton's men were exhausted and outnumbered by more than two to one, but he acted as he always did—boldly and audaciously. He sent a note to Buford demanding his surrender, telling the American that he was surrounded by a superior force. The American commander rejected Tarleton's proposal and replied that he and his men would resist the British advance. From his memoirs, it is clear that Tarleton was simply trying to delay the Americans—and in that he succeeded.[24]

The Americans set up a loose defensive position that was overrun by Tarleton's cavalry. Buford made a tactical error in ordering his men to withhold their fire until the British were almost upon them. After only one volley, the cavalry were in the American line and a terrible slaughter had begun. Tarleton attributed the carnage "to a report amongst the cavalry, that they had lost their commanding officer, which stimulated the soldiers to a vindictive asperity not easily restrained." Not only were men who tried to surrender cut down, but the wounded were bayoneted as they lay on the ground. One officer survived twenty-three stab wounds and the deliberate mistreatment of a British surgeon. At least 113 Americans were killed outright in Buford's Massacre, and another 150 wounded. Many of the wounded were so severely injured that they subsequently died.[25]

The mangled survivors were carried to the nearby Waxhaws

Church. The simple log structure was completely filled with wounded. Those local residents who had not fled in the face of the British advance did what they could to relieve the pain and suffering. Among those tending the wounded were Elizabeth Jackson and her two young sons, Andrew and Robert.[26]

The massacre at the Waxhaws did not have the impact that Tarleton and the British thought it would have. They assumed that the Scots-Irish would be intimidated by the might of British arms. Instead, *"Tarleton's quarter,"* wrote a nineteenth-century Presbyterian clergyman, "became a proverb for wholesale cruelty." When coupled with the general conduct of the British army and Clinton's revocation of paroles, many a Scots-Irish settler remembered the treachery of earlier Englishmen and decided that the time had come to resist. Andrew Jackson, just a lad of thirteen, joined Thomas Sumter's partisan band after helping his mother care for the survivors of Buford's Massacre. In New Acquisition District, William Hill and Andrew Neel rallied their fellow Scots-Irish.[27]

In early June, the British sent a former member of the General Assembly into the Waxhaws to convince the populace to surrender and become good British citizens. Hill's ironworks was the site chosen once again as the community meeting place. The Tory began to read a British proclamation averring that the Continental Congress had abandoned South Carolina and Georgia and that Washington and his army were in flight. Before he could finish, Hill stood up and said that the British proclamation was a bold-faced lie. He reminded his neighbors that "we has all taken an oath to defend & maintain the Independence of the state to the utmost of our power, we had one open side, we could keep in a body, go into North Carolina meet our friends & return with them to recover our State."[28]

The crowd's reaction was immediate. They sided with Hill,

and the Tory "was obliged to disappear with his proclamation and protections for fear of the resentment of the audience." The men agreed to form a new regiment and elected Hill and Andrew Neel as their colonels. Word spread about the formation of the unit, and men from Georgia and South Carolina joined up. Although other partisan leaders would become better known, William Hill was the first man in the backcountry after the fall of Charleston to rally the people to the American cause. Shortly afterward, William Bratton and Edward Lacey assembled a band of Whigs in the Catawba River Valley.[29]

When the newly organized militia learned of a Tory activity, it reacted quickly. Men from Lacey and Bratton's unit joined with Colonel Richard Winn and defeated Tory militia at Gibson's Meeting House and Brierley's Ferry. Neel led his men to the western portions of the New Acquisition in an attempt to capture a Tory recruiting officer and his recruits. The Tories escaped, and in going after them, Neel left the ironworks defended by only a dozen or so men.[30]

The British response to this unexpected stiffening of back-country resolve was another show of force. "I have taken the liberty," wrote Colonel George Turnbull to Cornwallis, "to order Captain Huck to destroy the Iron Works. They are the property of Mr. Hill, a great Rebell."[31]

On 11 June, a detachment of the British Legion commanded by Captain Christian Huck, a Philadelphia lawyer, rode into New Acquisition District to quash the incipient uprising. The eleventh was a Sunday, and as they rode into the area the legionnaires hoped to catch the Reverend John Simpson, the pastor of the Fishing Creek Church (Presbyterian) and an "ardent Whig." In the pulpit, when Simpson warmed to his subject, "he would break out with feeling bursts of eloquence, which, like an electric shock, never failed to move the hearts of his hearers." The cleric did more than just admonish his congregation to adhere to the American cause—he participated himself in the forcible disruption of several Tory gatherings.[32]

When the legionnaires arrived at the church, they found it empty and the good reverend nowhere to be found. Two days earlier, he had taken down his rifle and joined a local partisan band. Angry that their quarry had escaped, they murdered an unarmed local lad, who was shot while reading his Bible. Mrs. Simpson heard the shooting and hurried her four young children into a nearby thicket. After looting the parsonage, they burned it. They left Simpson's extensive library of Calvinist treatises in the house to be consumed by the flames.[33]

A week later, on 18 June, Huck's raiding party destroyed Hill's ironworks—one of their primary targets. The forge, the furnace, a gristmill, a sawmill, the residence, slave cabins, and other buildings were torched. The furnace's labor force of ninety slaves was carried away. The destruction of Hill's ironworks was of sufficient gravity for Governor Rutledge to inform the state's delegates to the Continental Congress.[34]

The British also considered the action at the Aera Furnace to be of considerable importance. On 30 June, Lord Cornwallis sent a report to General Clinton: "The capitulation of General [Andrew] Williamson at Ninety Six . . . and the dispersion of a party of rebels who had assembled at an iron works on the northwest border of the province . . . put an end to all resistance in South Carolina." Even as Cornwallis was writing his report, however, the British effort to pacify the South Carolina backcountry was running into difficulties.[35]

The plan that Clinton devised for Cornwallis to follow included the raising of militia units. All young and unmarried males in South Carolina, North Carolina, and Georgia were to be organized into companies of fifty to one hundred men. The companies would elect their own lieutenants, but a British officer would be assigned to each company "to provide discipline and order." These militia units would be an integral part of Cornwallis's force as he moved northward.[36]

Only in Ninety Six District did the British have much success in organizing Tory militia. In that district, it has been estimated, about fifteen hundred men in seven regiments saw duty from June to December 1780. Elsewhere, despite all their proclamations and threats, the British found recruiting difficult. They had an especially hard time locating officers—the best-qualified ones either had been or still were rebels.[37]

In the area along the North Carolina border known as the Pee Dee, Major James Wemyss was frustrated in his attempts to recruit a Tory regiment to be called the South Carolina Rangers. John Harrison was commissioned a major and given command of the unit. His two brothers, Robert and Samuel, were appointed as captains. None of these could be considered leading men in their communities, but they were the best officers that Wemyss could find. The rangers were supposed to have a complement of five hundred men, but they never numbered more than one hundred. And unfortunately for the British cause, they were more interested in loot and revenge than regular military action. Even Wemyss sometimes referred to his recruits as "banditti" and "plunderers." "Harrison's Corps" soon became a target for patriot militia units, and before the year was out all three Harrison brothers would be dead. Robert was killed in battle, and John and Samuel were shot while they slept in their beds.[38]

The conduct of the ill-disciplined rangers was not unusual. Cornwallis generally gave his subordinates such as Tarleton free rein. They, in turn, permitted Tory militia to "do what they please with the plantations abandoned by the rebels." Even though Cornwallis decreed that he would "severely punish any act of cruelty" perpetrated against the wives and children of rebels, such actions were all too common an occurrence.[39]

While Tarleton was in pursuit of Buford and Rutledge, he did not hesitate to take an opportunity to punish those he considered enemies of the king. On 28 May, as he approached the High Hills of the Santee, he intended to take as a prisoner Thomas Sumter, who had been a colonel in the Continental army. Sumter's eleven-year-old son was out riding when a neighbor warned him that Tarleton was looking for his father. The lad hurried home with the warning. Sumter put on his uniform and headed for Salisbury, North Carolina, where he knew there was an American army camp.

Two hours later, Tarleton's dragoons arrived at Sumter's plantation, which was located on high ground above the Santee River swamp. Mary Cantey Jameson Sumter, crippled since early childhood, was sitting on the porch of her home. Neither she nor her housekeeper were particularly cooperative. Mrs. Sumter refused to tell the British where her husband was. The housekeeper, when asked for the keys to the smokehouse, tossed them into the grass, but that did not deter the soldiers as they broke down the door and emptied the building of its contents. After taking whatever else they wanted from the house and barns, several carried Mrs. Sumter into the front yard. And as she watched, they set fire to her home.[40]

The actions of Tarleton's legion at Sumter's home were repeated many times by other British units operating in the backcountry. Wemyss, who, after Tarleton, was the most despised British officer in South Carolina, let his Tory rangers and his regular troops pretty much do whatever they wanted. They could plunder and burn homesteads and threaten women and children without any fear of being punished by their commander. Wemyss singled out Presbyterian churches for destruction, calling them "sedition shops." Even those who were disposed to be friendly to the king were appalled. Francis Kinloch, who was a very reluctant rebel, wrote to the former royal governor Thomas Boone that the actions of officers he knew "would make you and every worthy Englishman blush for the degeneracy of the Nation."[41]

Even when not pursuing a policy of intimidation, the British alienated Carolinians. Cornwallis's army had to be supplied. His officers were supposed to give certificates or receipts for food-stuffs, animals, or anything else taken. However, if they deemed a person to be a "decided enemy, and his character marked by acts of inhumanity towards loyalists," then his property was forfeit. In Camden, everything of Joseph Kershaw's was confiscated because Cornwallis deemed him "a violent man, [who] was said to have persecuted the loyalists." In Georgetown, Major Wemyss ignored his commander's policy. After declaring that the rice on nearby plantations was "part of the public stores and therefore legitimate prizes of war," he confiscated it.[42]

Cornwallis's report of 30 June was as uninformed as it was inac-curate. The policies that he and his subordinates were pursuing were counterproductive. The backcountry was like a giant hor-net's nest that had been poked, and the hornets were pouring out to punish those who had disrupted their lives, confiscated their property, and destroyed their homes and churches. Each British atrocity led to swift retaliation as life in the backcountry became a reign of terror for everyone. The British policy of intimidation and brutality had the opposite of the effect intended: instead of being cowed, the people of the South Carolina backcountry lashed out at their oppressors.[43]

Thomas Sumter had been content to remain on his plantation in the High Hills until Tarleton's men destroyed all he had. Their actions, wrote a nineteenth-century historian, "roused the spirit of the lion" and created an inveterate foe. Others who did not suffer any personal loss were nonetheless repelled by the callous and wanton cruelty of the occupying army.[44]

In New Acquisition District, after witnessing the destruction wrought by Captain Huck's troops, Daniel Collins returned home. When his wife asked him for the news, he replied, "Nothing very pleasant. I have come home determined to take my gun and when I lay it down, I lay down my life with it."[45]

In some families, it was the wife who convinced her husband to support the patriot cause. In the District Between the Broad and Catawba Rivers, Isabella Barber Ferguson had a heated confrontation with her brother-in-law, Colonel James Ferguson. "I am a rebel," she said. "My brothers are rebels, and the dog Trip is a rebel, too." She reminded her husband, Samuel, that they had discussed the matter many times and that there was no justification for the actions of the British and their Tory allies. "Now, in the presence of the British army," she warned, "if you go with them you may stay with them, for I can no longer be your wife." He did not join the Tory militia.[46]

The backcountry, especially the Catawba River Valley, was staunchly Presbyterian, and the influence of the clergy was considerable. The Reverend John Simpson had joined a patriot band in June. In the settlement at Rocky Creek, the Reverend William Martin was "a warm Whig and did not scruple to use his influence in the cause of the colonists." After the fall of Charleston and the movement of British troops into the area, the community was nervous. At eleven o'clock on a sabbath day early in June, the congregation was so large that they had to meet outdoors. It was as if they sensed that their minister was going to give them guidance.[47]

Only eight years earlier, Martin had led many of them from Ulster to South Carolina to escape the injustices of rapacious English landlords. Together they had built the log church at Rocky Creek. They were very much a community. As he rose to speak, there was a hushed silence. "My hearers, talk and angry words will do no good. *We must fight!*" He then explained that he had prayed and searched the scriptures and history in preparing that day's sermon. In the current "controversey between the United Colonies and the mother country," he had concluded that the Americans had been "forced to the declaration of their independence. Our forefathers in Scotland made a similar one and maintained that declaration with their lives; it is now our turn, brethren, to maintain this at all hazards."[48]

Martin recounted the events of the Revolution from 1776 to the present. As he began to detail what had happened in South Carolina since the fall of Charleston, his voice rose. Gesturing toward the Waxhaws, he thundered, "Go see the tender mercies of Great Britain! In that church you may find men, though still alive, hacked out of the very semblance of humanity; some deprived of their arms, some with one arm or leg, and some with both legs cut off. Is not this cruelty a parallel to the history of our Scottish fathers?"[49]

As was the custom, the service continued until well into the afternoon. There was little doubt that the men of the congregation would respond to their pastor's challenge. William Anderson and his wife, Nancy, talked on the way home. She said that she and their daughter could tend the crops while he went away to do his duty. He said that he was glad she felt that way because "[T]he way is now clear; the word of God approves." The next morning Anderson and other men in the community began to drill. Before the summer was out, William Anderson would fight in five battles and Nancy Stevenson Anderson would be a widow.[50]

Several days after Martin's sermon, some of Tarleton's legion attacked the militia as they drilled and others searched for the clergyman. They found him in his small home and took him prisoner. For months he was kept in chains in a jail in Rocky Mount and later in Camden for "preaching rebellion from the pulpit." The church at Rocky Creek, "a sedition shop," was burned.[51]

Within the space of ninety days, the British and their Tory allies had managed to turn the certain victory of mid-May into a very dicey situation. They controlled Charleston and strongholds across the state, but they did not control the countryside. The Tories' desire for revenge was understandable, but unwise—as was the gratuitous cruelty of Tarleton and Wemyss. On 22 May, Clinton had issued instructions to his officers that they were to keep the Tory militia under control "and by all means in your power protect the aged, the infirm, the women and children of every denomination from insult or outrage." Had the British officers in South Carolina followed their instructions in May and June 1780, they might not have found themselves facing a growing rebellion on the northern border of the state.[52]

By early July 1780, almost the entire border area from Georgetown to Spartan District, though temporarily occupied, was certainly not subdued. Clinton's revocation of paroles, the massacre at the Waxhaws, the plundering and destruction of innumerable homesteads, the mistreatment of women and children, and the studied hostility to the Presbyterian Church caused men and women to make the decision to fight for American independence. In 1780, as in past times of troubles, the residents of the backcountry looked to their community leaders. Whether they were men of property such as Thomas Sumter, William Hill, and William Bratton or men of the cloth such as John Simpson and William Martin, their opinions carried weight. Men were willing to follow their lead. In the summer of 1780, almost to a man, they came down on the side of resistance.[53]

4

The Tide Turns:
The Battle of Huck's Defeat

———•—•———

Good Lord, our God who art in heaven, we have reason to thank
Thee for the many favors received at Thy hands, the many battles
that have been won. There is one great and glorious battle at
King's Mountain where we kilt the great Gineral Ferguson and
took his whole army; and the great battles of Ramseur's and
Williamson's, and the ever memorable and glorious battle of the
Coopens where we made the proud Gineral Tarleton run doon the
road helter skelter; and Good Lord, if ye had na' suffered the
cruel tories to burn Billy Hill's iron works, we would na' have
asked any mair favors at thy hand. Amen.
PRAYER OF JOHN MILLER, A PRESBYTERIAN ELDER

By late June 1780, patriot bands were forming in the back-
country districts on both sides of the South
Carolina–North Carolina border. When Tarleton burned
his home, Thomas Sumter slipped across the border into North
Carolina and traveled to a small American army headquarters in
Salisbury. There he obtained permission to recruit and organize

militia units whose sole purpose would be to engage in a hit-and-run partisan campaign against the British army in South Carolina.[1]

Armed with this authority and some congressional Treasury certificates, Sumter established a camp in North Carolina at Tuckasegee Ford on the Catawba River. From his headquarters, he sent out word that all was not lost in South Carolina and called upon the residents of the backcountry to resist the British. In groups and as individuals, angry men from the Waxhaws, the New Acquisition, and Spartan District filtered into Sumter's camp. Among them were Richard Hampton from Spartan District and William Hill, William Bratton, and their neighbors from New Acquisition. Colonel George Turnbull, the commander of the British garrison at Rocky Mount on the Catawba River, wrote to Lord Cornwallis that "Cols. Patton, Bratton, Wynn, and a number of violent people have abandoned their habitations. It is believed they are gone amongst the Catawba Indians." The partisans were indeed on the Catawba Indian reservation, but they were not in hiding. They were members of Sumter's growing band of freedom fighters.[2]

There was no civil government in South Carolina. Governor Rutledge had barely escaped Tarleton's clutches and was in exile in North Carolina. Two of the three councillors who had escaped with him had turned themselves in and taken parole; the third was in Virginia. A startling number of the firebrands of the Revolution were dead, among them: Thomas Lynch Jr., signer of the Declaration of Independence; the Reverend William Tennent, champion of the backcountry and religious freedom; and William Henry Drayton, outspoken revolutionary idealist. A few military men, such as Francis Marion and Isaac Huger, had escaped the fall of Charleston, but they were lying low in coastal swamps. "The Revolutionary party," wrote a nineteenth-century historian, "was thus completely broken up."[3]

In the absence of established authority, these backcountry soldiers decided to select their own leaders. They could not be concerned about official commissions from the Continental Congress
or from Governor Rutledge. Their families were threatened and
they needed to act—just as they had done in the 1760s when outlaw bands were terrorizing the frontier.[4]

Initially, men from the New Acquisition put forth the names of
Colonel William Hill and Colonel William Bratton, but Colonel
Richard Winn of the District Between the Broad and Catawba
Rivers suggested that Colonel Thomas Sumter, the senior man
present, be elected. This proposal met with general assent, and
Sumter agreed to take command. After some consultation among
themselves (no doubt prompted by either Sumter or his allies),
the men decided that Sumter should be a brigadier general. In
accepting the position, he told those who had elected him: "Our
interests and fates are and must be identical. With me as with you
it is liberty or death."[5]

Sumter had a command, and he had the nucleus of a force to
oppose the British invasion, but despite the authority and paper
from Salisbury, the members of the newly formed partisan band
were on their own—and they knew it. In addition to electing their
leaders, the men agreed that they would provide their own
weapons, ammunition, food, and horses. According to Richard
Winn's memoirs, the men pledged to "oppose the British and
Tories by force of arms, which was never to be laid down until the
British troops was drove from the State of South Carolina and the
independence of the United States acknowledged."[6]

With a new camp on Clems Branch, just inside South Carolina,
Sumter's new command attracted a steady stream of new recruits
from the border districts. Some had been in uniform before. John
Adair, who had been at the surrender of Charleston, ignored his
parole and reenlisted. Henry Rea, a native of Ulster, had been in

and out of service since 1775. James Williams of Ninety Six District was an older soldier who had fought the Cherokee in 1776, but then gone back to his farm. In 1779 he wrote his son that he had been "obliged to take the field in defence of my rights and liberties, and that of my children." Fighting the British was not a matter of choice, "but of necessity, and from the consideration that I had rather suffer anything than lose my birthright, and that of my children."[7]

William Richardson Davie's family had moved to the Waxhaws in the mid-1760s; his uncle, William Richardson, was the pastor of the Waxhaws Church. After attending Princeton and reading for the law in Salisbury, North Carolina, Davie settled down there, in the upper reaches of the Catawba River Valley. Like many other Carolinians, he was in and out of uniform several times before 1780. His decision to reenter the service may have been spurred by news of Tarleton's massacre at the Waxhaws.[8]

Many were taking up arms for the first time. The Reverend John Simpson had left his pulpit just a step or two ahead of Tarleton's legion. Thomas McCalla, who had been in South Carolina for only about two years, decided that the time had come to fight. More than one-third of the men who would fight Captain Christian Huck and his legionnaires in July did not decide to join the patriot cause until 1780. A goodly number of these freedom fighters were under thirty. Colonel William Bratton was only twenty-seven. Thomas Gill and David Sadler were eighteen, and Joseph Gaston was a year younger.[9]

These frontier residents had usually witnessed firsthand the conduct of the British army that had ostensibly come to liberate them from those "wicked and desperate men" who were "still endeavouring to support the flame of rebellion." And if they had not suffered themselves, they knew of friends and neighbors who had. They, like the members of the Reverend John Simpson's congregation, were all too familiar with "the tender mercies of Great Britain."[10]

In the backcountry, news spread rapidly from one settlement to another. When Samuel and Isabella Ferguson had their discussion about the possibility that he would join a Tory militia unit, she mentioned the "unhallowed practices" of the British, who chained the Reverend Martin "by the feet like a felon."[11]

Most often news traveled by word of mouth, but occasionally it arrived by letter. From Sumter's camp, James Williams wrote to his wife, Mary, at Mount Pleasant in Little River: "I pray God that I may have the happiness of seeing you my love . . . in the course of a month, with a force sufficient to repel all the Tories in the upper part of South Carolina." After describing the growing strength of the patriot cause in the backcountry, he relayed to her the news of the burning of the Reverend John Simpson's "house and every thing he had." Williams, like many other men who had taken up arms, was concerned about his wife's safety. However, he was hopeful that their prayers "for each other and our bleeding country" would be joined in heaven.[12]

Williams did not mention their training, but for several weeks Sumter and his officers had been preparing their men to fight a new kind of warfare. Partisan, or guerrilla, warfare would require strength, endurance, and guile. Rather than work on parade-ground drilling—which was useless in the forests of the backcountry—the men engaged in something resembling an eighteenth-century version of today's ranger training. They ran, they swam, and they wrestled. They engaged in individual contests of strength and skill. By 4 July 1780, Sumter thought they were ready. He audaciously moved further into South Carolina and established a camp at Old Nation's Ford in the Catawba Indian reservation.[13]

As the number of men flocking to the cause of their "bleeding country" increased, the British became more uneasy. The uncertainty of the situation generated dozens of rumors. One of those rumors was that in New Acquisition District William Bratton was offering pardons to any loyalist who deserted his militia unit and joined the Americans. If true, Bratton's offer posed a threat to British strategy, which depended upon recruiting and employing a strong loyalist militia. Without loyalist militia units, the plan for rolling up the southern colonies would come unraveled.[14]

From the beginning, the British had overestimated the number of loyalists in the backcountry. Moreover, when they moved into the interior of the state, they encouraged their friends to harass their Whig neighbors. Instead of cowing Whigs and attracting those who had been neutral, the wanton vindictiveness and senseless cruelty of the Tory militia sparked fierce resistance. Overconfident and contemptuous of their opponents, the British did not seem to understand that their policies were creating far more problems than they were solving. Cornwallis took the position that "if those who say they are our own friends will not stir, I cannot defend every man's house from being plundered." And his lordship certainly had no intention of defending the houses of those who were not avowedly the king's friends.[15]

In Ninety Six District, George Park wrote to his cousin that, after the fall of Charleston and the disappearance of an American military presence, the Whig residents of the district were "like sheep among wolves" and the Whigs were "obliged to give up to them our Arms and take purtection." However, taking the king's protection provided none at all. No sooner had the dispirited residents taken protection than their Tory neighbors and British soldiers "set to Rob us taking all our living, horses, Cows, Sheep, Clothing, of all Sorts, money, pewter, tins, knives, in fine Everything that sooted them. Untill we were Stript Naked." James Williams had every reason to fear for his wife's safety in Tory-infested Ninety Six District.[16]

Backcountry Whigs frequently identified Tories as the "lower sort" who had associated with the outlaws in the 1760s. Among the prominent Tories was Joseph Coffel, who during that troubled time had finagled a commission from the royal governor to bring to justice several Regulators accused of breaking the law. Coffel immediately deputized men suspected of criminal activity. As he and his deputies moved into the backcountry, they arrested Regulators named in the governor's warrant and took the opportunity to pillage the settlements along the Saluda River. Law-abiding settlers were unwilling to accept this travesty of justice and prepared to fight Coffel and his men. Convinced of his error, the governor revoked Coffel's commission and the tensions eased—but backcountry residents had long memories.[17]

With the outbreak of the Revolution, Coffel chose to support the king in part because many of his personal enemies were Whigs. He was one of the most active recruiters on the frontier. As he had done during the 1760s, he recruited anyone willing to oppose the Revolution—and that included a good many men of questionable character, men on the margins of backcountry society. Because of Coffel's visibility, patriots began to use the derisive term "scoffelite" to describe their enemies. It was neither an accurate nor a fair description of the king's friends, but it nevertheless became widespread. One of the early historians of the Revolution in the state described backcountry Tories as "ignorant unprincipled banditti; to whom idleness, licentiousness and deeds of violence were familiar. Horse thieves and others whose crimes had exiled them from society attached themselves to the British." Unfortunately for the British, the conduct of Tory militia units reinforced the idea that they were indeed rogues and outlaws.[18]

British army units such as Banastre Tarleton's British Legion were just as callous and vindictive as their South Carolina militia allies. They had learned in just six weeks that the king had few friends in the Catawba River Valley. "[T]he Irish," noted Tarleton, "were the most averse settlers to the British government in America." The overwhelming majority of the settlers in the area were "Irish"—that is, Scots-Irish. Colonel George Turnbull, commander of the border garrison at Rocky Mount, learned that Bratton and "some of the violent rebels . . . had returned to their plantations, and were encouraging the people to join them." He ordered Captain Christian Huck to return to New Acquisition District to track down the rebels and to persuade those residents he encountered to be loyal to the king.[19]

Huck was a poor choice to lead an expedition into the heart of the Scots-Irish communities of the Catawba River Valley. His earlier incursion in June had been one of the primary causes of the very Whig activity that now concerned his superiors. Turnbull's instructions called for Huck "to proceed to the frontier of the Province collecting all the royal militia with you in your march, and with said forces to push the rebels as far as you may deem convenient." Huck needed little prodding, and during the first ten days of July he was determined to push the rebels as far and as hard as he could.[20]

The backcountry grapevine soon spread the word that Huck and a force of one hundred or so men were back in the New Acquisition. He had his men go to the houses in the area to summon all male residents to a meeting with their commander. There were no young men in the community, just a handful of aged men too old to fight. They had no choice but to appear. Once assembled, they were shocked and stunned at the captain's remarks. Frustrated that he had not been able to capture the Reverend Simpson in June, Huck told his listeners that it appeared that "God almighty had become a Rebel, but if there were 20 gods on that side, they would all be conquered." He was also reported to have said that "if the Rebels were as thick as trees, and Jesus Christ himself were to command them he would defeat them." While he was profanely haranguing the group, his soldiers confiscated the old men's horses, forcing them to walk back to their homes. As angry as the men and their families were at losing their horses, these devout Presbyterians were infuriated that Huck took the Lord's name in vain.[21]

Within a short time, news of Huck's blasphemy spread across the backcountry districts and set the tone for the rest of the captain's ill-fated expedition. Neither his offers of pardon and protection nor his threats of prison and death led to many new loyalist recruits. In fact, his words and actions resulted in just the opposite—the remaining men in the area slipped away to join the growing patriot companies. Huck's progress through the Catawba River Valley gave rise to stories of British brutality that quickly passed into folklore.[22]

At William Adair's home, Huck's men stripped the family of everything except the clothes on their backs. His wife, Mary Moore Adair, was rudely treated and robbed of her shoe buckles, rings, and a neckerchief. The legionnaires threatened to hang her husband and ordered her to send word to her two sons to forsake the rebel cause and join the king's friends. When patriot scouts came through a while later, Adair informed them that he could not offer them anything to eat because the British had taken all the foodstuffs from his larder and smokehouse. He told his friends that there was "not meal enough to make himself a hoe-cake."[23]

The roughing-up of backcountry women seemed to have been a common technique intended to intimidate them and their families. Many, however, were strong-willed, like Mary Moore Adair. They were not the least bit frightened by threats to them or their loved ones. Sometimes, if the accounts are accurate, these sturdy Scots-Irish housewives gave their tormentors a piece of their mind. Huck's actions kindled new accounts of British and Tory abuse that spread from house to house—no doubt sometimes exaggerated.

For example, when Huck's legionnaires had rampaged through the countryside a few weeks earlier, they not only looted the Reverend John Simpson's home but went out of their way to insult his wife. Several of the Tory raiders appropriated the clergyman's clothes and took great delight in taunting Mrs. Simpson. Surely, they mocked her, the clothes looked better on them than they had on her husband. They assured her that she would never see him alive again, and one legionnaire vowed to bring her his scalp. News of these British outrages did not have the effect their perpetrators thought they would. Instead of intimidating the inhabitants, such incidents hardened their resolve.[24]

Some British officers in the backcountry complained that the South Carolinians deliberately distorted the truth to stir up the populace. From Rocky Mount, Turnbull informed Cornwallis that rumors circulating in the Catawba River Valley had done incalculable damage. Accounts of British atrocities—real, exaggerated, or fabricated—were effective patriot propaganda. The New Acquisition, with its predominantly Scots-Irish population, was the only district in South Carolina where virtually none of the residents agreed to take British protection.[25]

Captain John McClure was one of a handful of partisan leaders on Christian Huck's most-wanted list. McClure and his wife, Mary, were members of the Reverend John Simpson's congregation at Fishing Creek. While her husband was away with Sumter's band, Mary McClure did what she could to support the patriot cause. On 11 July, when Huck's men approached the McClure homestead, they hoped to capture John. He was not there, but the legionnaires did surprise two other partisans, the McClures' son James and their son-in-law Edward Martin.[26]

Both men were members of Sumter's band. They and their fellows had agreed that they would furnish their own weapons and ammunition. Shot was in short supply, but Mary McClure did have a number of pewter dishes and utensils. McClure and Martin were melting down the pewter and making bullets when the British rode up to the house. Surprised, they tried to hide. Unfortunately for them, the legionnaires were intent on cleaning out the place, as they had the Adairs'. Both partisans were quickly discovered. The British found the molten pewter and bullet molds. When they searched the two men, they found newly molded bullets in their pockets. The bullets, along with the molten pewter and bullet molds, were more than sufficient evidence for Huck to condemn the Carolinians as "violent rebels" and traitors. He immediately ordered the men placed under guard and decreed that they be hanged at sunrise the next day. When Mrs. McClure protested the captain's decision, one of his men struck her with the flat of his sword.[27]

In the confusion, the British failed to realize that there was another person in the house. According to family tradition, the daughter of the house—also named Mary McClure—eluded her family's tormentors and rode to Sumter's camp. There she told her father and brothers of Huck's latest outrages.[28]

Besides McClure, the British were determined to find William Hill and William Bratton. Huck's earlier foray into the area had left the Hill family homeless, and they were in hiding in the woods. Bratton's plantation was intact and became the legionnaires' next target.

Warned by their neighbors, Martha Robertson Bratton and her six-year-old son, William, waited with some trepidation for the enemy to appear. In his later account of the incident, the younger Bratton wrote: "At last they were seen coming up the road, a long line of Redcoats, followed by a great crowd of Tories." A squad detached itself from the main body and approached the house. Martha Bratton, with her young son at her side, met them on the front porch and asked what they wanted. They told her that they were seeking her husband and asked whether he was home. She replied that not only was he not home, but she did not know where he was. Her response infuriated a "red-headed ruffian," who cursed and said that he would make her talk. A reaping hook was hanging on a peg on the front wall. The Tory militiaman grabbed it and drew his sword. With the reaping hook at her throat, he threatened to cut off her head if she did not reveal Colonel Bratton's whereabouts.[29]

There are several different accounts of Martha Bratton's reply to her inquisitors. All, however, depict her stance as cool and brave. According to one source, when asked where her husband was, she proudly stated: "In Sumter's army." In a rage, the Tory used the reaping hook to try to frighten her into revealing her husband's whereabouts. William Bratton's version does not have his mother verbally defy the British until the incident with the reaping hook. Then, with the blade at her throat, in "deliberate and measured tones" she is reported to have said: "I told the simple truth and could not tell if I would; but I now add, that I would not if I could."[30]

Because of her insolence, Martha Robertson Bratton courted death. To the revenge-minded Tory militia or the hardened veterans of the British Legion, such an act would not have generated a second thought. To them the only good rebel was a dead one— and rebels were rebels regardless of age or gender. Just when it seemed that the man was going to carry out his threat, he was struck by one of his own officers. The sword and reaping hook clattered to the floor. With his sword drawn, a Tory captain, John Adamson of Camden, stood over the downed man. He proceeded to beat the attacker with the flat of his sword and then kicked him off the porch. The captain apologized to Mrs. Bratton and assured her that she and her family would not be harmed. Without a word, she went inside with her son holding fast to her skirts.[31]

Later Huck himself rode up to the Brattons' house and

demanded that Mrs. Bratton prepare a meal for him and his officers. This she did. Then she and her children retreated up the
enclosed stairway to the second floor of their home. Three elderly
neighbors who had been visiting—Thomas Clendennen, John
"Gum Log" Moore, and Charles Curry—were taken prisoner.
These men, like John McClure and Edward Martin, were told
that they would be executed the next day. For some reason,
Huck's men did not set fire to the Bratton homestead when they
left. There were hints, however, that they would return the next
day.[32]

Huck then moved on about a half-mile down the road to James
Williamson's plantation. Very likely the place was abandoned, as
there were no reported incidents. All of the men in the household
were partisans (all five Williamson sons were serving with Bratton). The comfortable plantation looked like the perfect place to
spend the night. So Huck and his force of 115 men (35 dragoons of
the British Legion, 20 New York Volunteers, and 60 local Tories)
made their camp. The prisoners were locked up in a corncrib to
await their execution.[33]

After the British departed, Martha Bratton sent her slave Watt
to go find her husband. If stopped, he was to say that he was looking after the cows, which, like most farm animals in the backcountry, ranged freely in the nearby woods. Watt located Bratton at
Fishing Creek and informed him of all that had transpired. Most
important, he told his owner where Huck and his detachment had
pitched their camp.[34]

Later that evening a third messenger arrived with intelligence
about the British camp. Joseph Kerr had been crippled since birth,
but he nonetheless joined the militia. Because he could not fight,
he served his unit as a spy on three separate occasions. He wan-
dered into the legionnaires' camp on the morning of 11 July and
kept his eyes and ears open. Several local Tories accused him of

being a rebel, but his protestations and his physical condition protected him. Nevertheless, Captain Huck ordered him to remain with his force throughout the day. After the British had bedded down for the night, he managed to escape on horseback and find his own partisan band.[35]

Kerr was able to give the patriots a layout of Huck's camp. It was near a substantial, two-story log house along the road. A sturdy split-log fence surrounded the house and lined the road on both sides. Some of the detachment were sleeping in an open field; others had pitched their tents along the road. Huck and several officers were in the house. Security was very loose. As Cornwallis later reported to Clinton, "Captain Huck, encouraged by meeting no opposition, encamped in an unguarded manner." Incredibly, in an area noted for its support of the Revolution, no outlying pickets or roving patrols were posted to provide an early warning of hostile activity. "Captain Huck," concluded Tarleton, "neglected his duty, in placing his party carelessly at a plantation." Kerr gave his fellows all these details and then volunteered to lead them back to the campsite.[36]

The several accounts of the battle at Williamson's plantation are varied and sometimes differ in detail. That disparity is understandable because, despite Sumter's election as a general and his acknowledged leadership abilities, there were independent partisan bands operating throughout the Catawba River Valley. After receiving word that Huck had returned to harass their community, Captain John McClure and Colonel William Bratton, with about 150 volunteers, left Sumter's camp in pursuit. Captain Edward Lacey and Colonels Andrew Neel and William Hill, learning of Huck's whereabouts, also were tracking him.[37]

En route the Americans passed William Adair's home, where Adair recounted Huck's recent visit. He also warned the partisans that they would be facing a British-Tory force of nearly one thousand. The exaggerated figure did not deter the partisans. They were determined to punish Huck for what he had done to their community.[38]

Initially there were about 500 men in three or four loosely organized partisan bands. Through a mix-up in communications, some 150 men headed off in the opposite direction toward Charlotte. Not all of them were on horseback, and another hundred or so fell out. By the time the South Carolinians reached Bratton's place, there were perhaps a few more than 250 men. All of the leading patriots in the neighborhood were present: Bratton, Hill, McClure, Neel, and Lacey.[39]

Edward Lacey had to deal with an unusual security problem. His family farm was only two miles from Williamson's, and his father was a die-hard Tory. The elder Lacey made it clear to his son that he had every intention of revealing the partisans' plans to Huck. Despite being guarded by four men, the old man somehow managed to slip out of the house and headed for Huck's camp. His escape was discovered immediately, and he was captured before he had gone more than several hundred yards. This time, to ensure the safety of the mission, Captain Lacey had his father tied to his bedstead to prevent him from warning the British.[40]

The elder Lacey's contact was very probably his other son, Reuben, who was serving with the Tory militia under Huck's command. Reuben was a notorious slacker and suffered from poor eyesight. According to local tradition, several partisan scouts saw a lone rider heading their way. It was Reuben Lacey. Clouds darkened the moon, and with his impaired vision he could not identify the men who challenged him. During the exchange, the partisans said they were friends of the king but had lost their way. They then inquired about the location of Huck's camp and the position of the sentinels so they could safely enter the camp. The trusting Tory told them everything they asked, including the precise location of four sentries. The partisans then let the poor man pass and quickly relayed this crucial information back to the other Americans.[41]

Bratton knew the countryside well and concealed his men in a nearby swamp. After checking to see that his family was safe, he reconnoitered the area. He quickly discovered the lax security. Just as Joseph Kerr had said, there were no patrols. There were four sentries, but they were not particularly alert. The colonel easily passed between the sentries and carefully reconnoitered the bivouac area. It appeared that all of the off-duty soldiers were asleep in their tents. Obviously no one in the British camp had any idea that the partisans were in the vicinity.[42]

When Bratton returned from his one-man patrol, there was a council of war. The Americans would divide their force. Bratton would lead one group of partisans down the road from his place toward Williamson's plantation. Lacey would lead the other. His band would circle around the British site and attack on the road from the other side. Just before the battle, another partisan band commanded by Captain John Moffett of the District Between the Broad and Catawba Rivers appeared and agreed to attack the British from a third side.[43]

As the darkness waned, the patriots, on horseback, rode toward the enemy camp from three directions. The plan called for Bratton and Lacey to attack simultaneously from either end of the country road that ran in front of the house—and right through the middle of the British camp. Moffett's men would use the cover of a peach orchard to move in on the rear of the house.[44]

"Not long after sunrise," wrote James Collins, one of Moffett's men, "we came in sight of their headquarters, which were in a log building. The men dismounted in the orchard and advanced on foot. A sentry saw movement and fired at the approaching partisans. He then retreated back to the main camp to sound the alarm. Some of the legionnaires were able to mount their horses and move against the attackers. With the peach trees as conceal-ment, the Americans began firing. One of the British officers (quite possibly Huck himself) yelled, "Disperse you damned rebels, or I will put every man of you to the sword."[45]

Along the road the attack did not proceed as planned. In maneuvering around the British camp, Lacey's men had to tra-verse swampy terrain. They killed the sentry on their side of the camp, but Bratton's men had already launched their attack before Lacey's men were in place.[46]

When Bratton's men were within seventy-five paces of the enemy, they opened fire. There was pandemonium in the camp as soldiers struggled from their tents. A Tory officer wrote that the rebels caught them totally by surprise and were in the camp before the British knew what was happening. Although the fence was made of split rails, it afforded the partisans some cover and concealment. It also provided them with a solid rest for their rifles, "with which they took unerring and deadly aim." The legion-naires, at last aroused to the danger, tried to break through the patriot ranks with bayonet attacks. Normally this was one of the British tactics that the Americans feared most. This time, how-ever, the Carolina militia withstood three bayonet charges. It was the British and Tories who broke and ran, not the rebels.[47]

Captain Huck compounded his earlier negligence by not real-izing the gravity of his situation. The battle was well under way before he emerged from Williamson's house. Mounting his horse, he rode back and forth behind the lines urging his men to rally for one more charge. Thomas Carroll, one of Moffett's sharp-shooting backcountrymen, put two balls in Huck's head, right behind his ear. The captain dropped his sword and fell from his saddle. When he hit the ground, the remaining legionnaires and Tories panicked. Sensing the flow of the battle, the cry went up from the partisans along the road: "Boys take the fence, and every man his own commander!"[48]

As the partisans rushed into the camp, resistance collapsed. Some Tories threw down their weapons and begged for mercy. Others fled into the woods. The Americans took to their horses and "pursued the flying loyalists for thirteen or fourteen miles, wreaking vengeance and retaliating for their cruelties and atrocities."[49]

Within an hour, the battle itself was over. Colonel Richard Winn noted: "The enemies' loss, killed, wounded and prisoners, was considerable, besides, about one hundred horses, saddles, bridles, pistols, swords, and many other things." William Hill reported that the British casualties included Huck; his lieutenant, who "was wounded and died afterwards; considerable number of privates the number is not known, as there were many carcasses found in the woods some days after." Lacey's biographer reported that "many of the wounded Tories escaped into the woods, and were afterwards found dead." Joseph Kerr said that ninety-eight men of the British Legion and Tory militia were killed. Tarleton reported that only twenty-four men escaped, meaning that ninety-one were killed or captured. The losses—even if not the 85 percent killed in action that Kerr reported—were appalling.[50]

Hill's comment that "there were many carcasses found in the woods some days after" does not leave much to the imagination. Members of Tarleton's legion and their Tory militia allies undoubtedly received "Tarleton's quarter." The pursuit of the survivors was "ruthless." The killing of wounded or unarmed foes was fast becoming an accepted tactic in the South Carolina backcountry, one employed by both Americans and British. In May 1780, Banastre Tarleton had unleashed a cycle of bloody retribution that would not cease until the war was over.[51]

Later historians reported that the partisans gave quarter to all but one man, an individual accused of murdering William Strong.

The battle's participants remembered the aftermath of the battle differently. So, too, did young William Bratton. He recalled seeing his father and others preparing to hack a wounded Tory to pieces.[52]

Throughout the night, Martha Bratton and her children had huddled in the second story of their home. As the Tories retreated down the Lincoln Road past the house, there was considerable gunfire all around. Mrs. Bratton made her son sit in the fireplace for protection against stray shots. Several penetrated their sanctuary, but no one was injured.[53]

Once it was daylight and the shooting had stopped, the Brattons left the safety of their home and went outside. There were enemy wounded lying all about. A short distance from the house William Bratton saw his father and Captain John Chambers standing with their drawn swords over a fallen British officer. They asked Martha Bratton whether she recognized the man. She said that she did not, and then, with great difficulty, the man spoke. He had suffered a severe puncture wound in his chest and had lost a great deal of blood, but she instantly recognized the voice. He had requested that she be sent for, "more to save your husband from a cruel injustice to himself than from any service you may be able to render me."[54]

The wounded Tory was John Adamson, the officer who had saved her life the previous afternoon. As the Carolinians were clearing the battlefield, Colonel Bratton was searching for the Tory who had assaulted his wife, and he believed that the wounded officer was the guilty party. When the man denied the accusation, he was accused of cowardice, of trying to hide behind Mrs. Bratton's skirts. Then Bratton and Chambers "drew their swords to cut him into mincemeat." As they did so, Adamson gasped: "It is of little consequence to me, sir, for you can only hasten the end, which I feel is fast approaching; but I beg of you to consult Mrs. Bratton before you perpetrate so great a wrong." Something in the wounded man's tone of voice caused Bratton to hold back and send for his wife.[55]

Once Martha Bratton identified her rescuer, those who had intended to execute him carried him into the house for treatment. The first floor of the Bratton residence was filled with enemy wounded and dying. To make space for Adamson, others had to be moved. "I remember well," said young William Bratton, "how [John] Adair and another man took up Redcoats, one by the head and the other by the heels, and threw them out of the house like dead hogs." When Mrs. Bratton protested, they just laughed at what they considered her misplaced concern for the enemy wounded. As for Adamson, although everyone (himself included) thought he was dying, thanks to the tender care he received from Martha Bratton he recovered and lived many years after the Revolution.[56]

Mary Moore Adair and several other women in the area helped Martha Bratton nurse the wounded. Among them was a Tory captain who the evening before had directed that she tell her sons to give themselves up. As she dressed his wounds, she chided him: "Well, captain, you ordered me to bring in my rebel sons. Here are two of them; and if the third had been within a day's ride, he would have been here also." The Tory acknowledged that he had indeed seen them—unfortunately, in the thick of the battle.[57]

Although there was great carnage on the British side, American casualties were negligible. Just one Carolinian was killed, and one wounded. Because of the swift and successful dawn attack, the planned executions of the five rebel prisoners had not occurred. After the battle, they were released from their corncrib jail unharmed.[58]

The battle at Williamson's plantation was a tremendous triumph for the Americans. There had been little good military news in South Carolina since the beginning of the year. The victory "was the first check the enemy had received after the fall of Charleston," wrote William Hill, "and was of greater consequence than can well be supposed from an affair of [so] small a magnitude—as it had the tendency to inspire the Americans with courage and fortitude & teach them that the enemy was not invincible."[59]

The impact of the battle—which soon became widely known as "Huck's Defeat"—was immediate. The entire backcountry seemed to take heart. Frontier militia had defeated soldiers of the feared British Legion. Only a few days after the battle, new volunteers swelled the ranks of Sumter's band to more than six hundred men. Tory militia units began to fall away. A commander in one Tory regiment led his entire battalion into Sumter's camp— along with the arms and ammunition they had been supplied by the British. With the dwindling presence of Tory militia, the depredations against Whig communities declined.[60]

The name that backcountry folk chose to give the battle had significance. Every time the story of the clash was told, it underscored the defeat of British provincial regulars by partisans defending their community. "The enemy," as William Hill noted, "were not invincible." It was a lesson that would have an impact on the course of the Revolution in South Carolina.

The Battle of Huck's Defeat was Cornwallis's first setback in South Carolina. It occurred less than two weeks after he had confidently reported to Clinton that "the dispersion of a party of rebels who had assembled at an iron works on the north-west border of the province . . . put an end to all resistance in South Carolina." Clearly the state of South Carolina might be occupied, but its people had not been conquered—especially not those living along the northwest border of the province. From Spartan District in the piedmont to Georgetown on the coast, the British and Tories were on the defensive—but nowhere were the partisans more aggressive than in the Catawba River Valley. There, in the Waxhaws and the New Acquisition, the Scots-Irish were encouraged by their clergy to resist in something akin to a holy war. They enthusiastically rallied behind Bratton, Hill, and McClure and joined with Sumter's partisans to fight the British and Tories at every turn.[61]

5

July–October 1780:
The Beginning of the End

The unlucky affair that happened to the detachment of Captain
Christian Huck of the Legion has given me great uneasiness.
LORD CORNWALLIS

The British army of occupation in South Carolina (regulars and provincial troops) numbered about 4,000 men. More than three-fourths of them were needed to garrison key towns and forts scattered across the state. Along the border with North Carolina there were nearly 1,200 men in four outposts: Fairforest (30), Rocky Mount (200), Hanging Rock, and Cheraw (600). Another 1,500 were stationed at other backcountry strongholds. If Great Britain's grand southern strategy was to succeed, Cornwallis had to be able to recruit and retain a large number of Tory militia units to augment his forces and assist with the occupation and pacification of the state.[1]

The number of potential loyal recruits was never as large as the British had hoped it would be. Now, with the beginnings of an armed insurgency in the backcountry, those who had flocked to the Union Jack in May and June 1780 began to have second thoughts. The British commander had every reason to feel uneasy about what "happened to the detachment of Captain Christian Huck of the Legion."

If ragtag rebel bands were willing to challenge the feared British Legion, they would have no hesitation in taking on Tory militia units. Not only did Huck's Defeat give the patriots a tremendous psychological boost, it caused Tories—and would-be Tories—to reconsider their collaboration with the British. Colonel Nesbit Balfour, commander of the garrison at Ninety Six, wrote that the rebel victories at Williamson's plantation and Ramseur's Mill (North Carolina) had had an impact on the military situation along the northern frontier. "I find the enemy exerting themselves wonderfully and successfully in stirring up the people," he wrote. "Many that had protection have already joined them. . . . They have terrified our friends."[2]

From the stronghold at Fairforest, Major Patrick Ferguson wrote that the rebels were "undoubtedly in very high spirits" after Huck's Defeat. Ferguson echoed Balfour's analysis that after the battle at Williamson's plantation the rebels "had begun to make risings in small partys on the frontier."[3]

There were numerous "small risings" and skirmishes all over the backcountry. The "small partys" might be only a handful of men on either side—or they might be a larger force. Many of these engagements were never recorded, and the participants and the outcomes have been lost to history. However, between Huck's Defeat on 12 July and the great battle at King's Mountain on 7 October, there were some twenty-two engagements involving partisan bands and their enemies. Seventeen of these encounters occurred in the backcountry.[4]

Six of these battles took place in the two weeks after Huck's Defeat. Each was an independent action fought by local partisans. With each one, support for the American cause in South

Carolina increased. A modern military historian has written that these engagements were not major battles, but that their cumulative effect—and the personnel losses suffered by the British—were significant. American casualties were less than one-half those of their enemy, but they could be replaced. The British losses could not.[5]

On 12 July, the very day that Huck was defeated at Williamson's plantation, there was another battle in New Acquisition. Captain Thomas Brandon, a Scots-Irishman from Fairforest in Spartan District, had a deep, burning hatred of his Tory neighbors. It is not known why this was so, but all accounts describe him in this manner. Perhaps Brandon's temper had been forged earlier in the summer when a Tory prisoner escaped from his camp and revealed its position. Brandon's little band was surprised and routed. Several partisans died, but most escaped. In the months that followed, Brandon displayed no compassion for any Tory unfortunate enough to fall into his hands.[6]

Brandon's intense feelings were not unique, and in nineteenth-century fiction they were ascribed to many a patriot. For example, in Simms's *Jocelyn*, a partisan warns a Tory to get out of the country: "If you remain here long . . . I would not give a shilling for your life." In his band, Brandon had men whose loathing for Tories equaled his own.[7]

Learning that a group of Tories had created a fortified post at Stallions, a farmstead on Fishing Creek (just a few miles from Williamson's plantation), Brandon decided that they had to be eliminated. He gathered a raiding party of about fifty Whigs and set out for Stallions. As they approached the makeshift fort, he decided to attack the Tories from the front and the rear. Brandon and some thirty men maneuvered around to the back of the property while a Captain Love and sixteen men moved in on the front.[8]

Thomas Young, a member of Love's detachment, left an eye-witness account. As the Americans approached, Mrs. Stallions (who was Captain Love's sister) heard them and ran out to meet the partisans. She pleaded with her brother not to attack and then, when her entreaties failed, ran back to her house. As she reached the doorway of the cabin, shots rang out from the opposite side. A stray bullet came through the rear door and killed her instantly.[9]

"At the moment with Brandon's attack," wrote Young, "our party raised a shout and rushed forward. We fired several rounds, which were briskly returned." Outnumbered and surrounded, the Tories attempted to surrender. One of them "ran up a flag, first upon the end of a gun; but, as that did not look exactly peaceful, a ball was put through the fellow's arm, and, in a few minutes, the flag was raised on a ramrod, when we ceased firing."[10]

In the heat of the battle, Young saw a man running away through a cornfield. He raised his rifle to his shoulder, but one of his compatriots told him to hold his fire because the runner was "one of our own men." A moment or two later, the man turned and fired on the partisans. Retaliation was swift and lethal. A rifle shot brought down the man. He was one of thirty-four Tory casualties at Stallions: two killed, four wounded, and twenty-eight prisoners of war. The POWs were sent to Charlotte for internment. Stallions, the owner of the property, "was dismissed, on parole, to bury his wife and arrange his affairs." Young reported that the bereaved husband and his brother-in-law shed "bitter tears" over their mutual loss. The Americans suffered one man wounded.[11]

While the fighting was raging in the New Acquisition, Jane Black Thomas was tending her ill sixty-year-old husband, who was a prisoner of war in Ninety Six. Colonel John Thomas Sr. was the organizer and first commander of the Spartan Regiment. He had participated in the Snow Campaign of 1775 and the Cherokee

Campaign of 1776. Following the fall of Charleston, he had surrendered. However, when Clinton issued his infamous 3 June
1780 proclamation, Thomas once again took up arms against the
British. He was arrested and incarcerated in the stockade at
Ninety Six. After his arrest, the men of the regiment elected his
son, John Thomas Jr., as their commander.[12]

On the evening of 12 June, Jane Thomas overheard several
Tory women discussing a planned raid on the headquarters of the
Spartan Regiment at Cedar Springs in Spartan District. In addition to John Jr., she had several other sons, friends, and neighbors
in the unit. As soon as it was light, the intrepid woman got on her
horse and rode more than fifty miles to warn her son and some
sixty of his men.[13]

After a brief discussion of what they should do, the Americans
decided to withdraw from their camp. They left their tents up and
campfires burning. During the night, a force of 150 Tories
approached the campsite at Cedar Springs. Sensing the opportunity to quash the insurgents in Spartan District, they wasted no
time on strategy. They immediately rushed headlong into the
camp, intent on dispatching the partisans while they slept. Silhouetted against the firelight, the Tories were easy targets for the
backcountry sharpshooters concealed in the surrounding woods.
"The engagement," wrote a nineteenth-century historian, "was
short, quick and decisive." Because of the darkness, the Tories
were unsure of the size of the force they faced. Concerned that
they might be trapped, they retreated, leaving several of their
wounded and dead behind. Realizing their perilous situation if
they remained in the neighborhood, the outnumbered partisans
withdrew into North Carolina.[14]

About one-third of the defeated Tories retreated twenty miles
to Gowen's Old Fort on the South Pacolet River. Located on the
border between Spartan District and what had been Cherokee

lands, the "fort" was probably one of a number of strong log houses built originally for defense against the Indians. Furious at being ambushed, the Tories prepared to ride into North Carolina after Thomas and his band. They sent out scouts to bring in additional recruits.[15]

One of these scouts came across a group of Georgia and South Carolina partisans who were trying to join up with Sumter or others still willing to resist the British. The Georgians had crossed the Savannah River into Ninety Six District—a hotbed of loyalist sentiment. Their commander decided that the British had the upper hand and that it might be more sensible to return to their homes and wait for a more opportune time to fight. More than 100 of the 140 men agreed and withdrew back across the Savannah. Joined by several South Carolinians, the remaining partisans pressed forward.[16]

To safely cross the western portions of South Carolina, the Whigs now passed themselves off as loyalists. On more than one occasion, local Tories, believing the deception, actually guided them toward the North Carolina line. Sometime on 13 July, they met up with one of the Tory scouts from Gowen's Old Fort. Feigning sympathy, they readily agreed to join in the pursuit of the victors at Cedar Springs. The recruiting scout led the partisans right back to Gowen's Old Fort.[17]

It was nearly midnight when the patriots arrived at the campsite. Security was slack, and most of the loyalists were asleep. Stealthily surrounding the camp, the partisans opened fire on their enemies. The fighting was over in a matter of minutes. The groggy, surprised loyalists shouted for quarter. In this instance, it was granted. One loyalist was killed, three were wounded, and thirty-two were taken prisoner. The prisoners were paroled, but one of the Tory scouts was impressed to guide the partisans to Earle's Ford on the North Pacolet River in the upper reaches of

Spartan District. There they met up with Colonel Charles McDowell of North Carolina, who was on the trail of Major Patrick Ferguson.[18]

Ferguson, a British army officer, commanded a mixed force of loyalist regulars and local militia. Like Tarleton, Ferguson was determined to do whatever it took to defeat the rebels. While he was moving through the lower portion of Spartan District, Joseph Kerr, the crippled spy, was able to ferret out British intentions and get word to McDowell.[19]

Although McDowell now knew Ferguson's whereabouts, he was in no position to do anything about it. His men were exhausted after a forced march to the banks of the North Pacolet River. The Georgians, too, were tired after their trek and the skirmish at Gowen's Old Fort. McDowell, rather than push his newly augmented command unnecessarily, decided that it would be prudent to rest for a day or so before setting off again. Ferguson was not in the immediate vicinity, and the local Tories seemed to have scattered. Just to be sure, McDowell sent a scouting party to the opposite (western) side of the river. When the scouts did not return by dark, the partisans assumed that they were safe in their bivouac on high ground overlooking a ford in the river.[20]

Assumptions are always dangerous—especially in a military situation. McDowell's scouts had not returned because they were lost. Because of the location of the camp and the apparent absence of enemy forces, no pickets were posted across the river. While the weary partisans slept, a troop of fourteen dragoons plus some sixty loyalist militia were doggedly tracking the Georgia Whigs who had humiliated the Tories at Gowen's Old Fort. Major James Dunlap, a regular army officer, was in command.[21]

Dunlap's men were part of the garrison at Prince's Fort, one of the many upcountry retreats built during the Cherokee War. Located in Spartan District along the old Indian frontier line, the circular structure was built of heavy timbers twelve to fifteen feet high. Dirt was piled against the wall and abatis (sharpened stakes) stuck into it. Beyond the walls the land was cleared to provide open fields of fire and to prevent sneak attacks. From such a stronghold a few British soldiers and local Tory militia could terrorize the neighborhood.[22]

During the middle of the night of 15 July, Dunlap's force reached the west bank of the Pacolet. He thought that the camp across the river contained only the Georgia partisans and figured that with his superior numbers he would crush the rebels. As the British began to ford the river, several of the partisans awoke to the danger and gave the alarm, but it was too late. The dragoons rode into the midst of the patriot camp.[23]

The Georgians were closest to the river and took the brunt of the attack. Men were killed as they slept. The Tory militia dismounted and began systematically to butcher every partisan they encountered. Noah Hampton, son of Captain Edward Hampton, was with McDowell's men. Awakened by the firing, he was captured as he tried to reach his weapon. When asked his name, he replied proudly: "Hampton." After cursing him and his family for treason, the Tories bayoneted the unarmed youth to death. Several other partisans suffered the same fate.[24]

But the battle was far from over. The remaining Whigs retreated and formed a defensive position at the top of the rise. Then, under orders from McDowell and Hampton, they moved forward. Dunlap, realizing that he had underestimated the size of the American force, retreated across the river. The battle at Earle's Ford (sometimes called McDowell's Camp) was over. The partisans suffered eight killed and thirty wounded; eight of the British were killed. Despite the number of casualties, Carolinians considered the battle a victory. Dunlap's mission had been to eliminate the rebel forces in the area, and in that he had failed. By leaving the field to the partisans, the British left themselves and their Tory allies open to retaliation. Within hours, Dunlap would rue his decision.[25]

Edward Hampton was an angry man. He was livid that his commander (McDowell) had been so lackadaisical about posting sentries. He made his feelings known, but there was little that he could do about past errors of judgment. There was something he could do to punish the Tories for the murder of his son. The callous and savage stabbing of Noah and his unarmed fellows as they asked for quarter called for revenge.[26]

McDowell ordered a raiding party of fifty-two mounted partisans to pursue the enemy and inflict whatever damage they could. The best horses in the camp were made available, and Edward Hampton was named commander. He was a logical choice because he was from the area and knew the terrain. But by giving him the command, McDowell also provided the grieving father with an opportunity to avenge his son's death.[27]

The British were incredibly easy to track. After the battle, they had initially remained in the general area well into the morning. Then, at a leisurely pace, they headed back toward their headquarters at Prince's Fort. They traveled on well-marked roads and stopped several times to rest. Had they moved out immediately, it would have been difficult, if not impossible, for the partisans to catch them. As it was, in a matter of two hours Hampton's men covered fifteen miles and completely surprised the enemy. Eight of Dunlap's troop fell in the first onslaught. Panic set in. Abandoning their horses and much of their gear, the British fled down the road for the safety of the fort. The partisans chased them, killing several more before halting just outside range of the fort's guns.[28]

Hampton lost not a man in this skirmish near Prince's Fort. He returned to McDowell's Camp "with thirty-five good horses, dragoon equipage, and a considerable portion of the enemy's baggage as trophies of the victory." The enemy dead were left where they fell. One Tory corpse lay for several days near a giant oak by the roadside. No family came to claim the body, and incensed Whigs did not consider the fallen loyalist worthy of a decent burial. Finally, after the body had lain for several days in the July sun, several nearby residents decided that the bloated remains had to be disposed of. So they dug a hole and rolled the Tory's body into it—disposing of their enemy as they would any farm animal.[29]

On 15–16 July 1780, the British failed in their attempt to eliminate the "small partys" of rebels that were resisting their efforts to subdue Spartan District. Although the Whigs had suffered thirty-eight casualties at Earle's Ford, they repulsed the enemy attack. Then Hampton's band tracked down and surprised Dunlap's force near Prince's Fort. The Americans returned to their camp, but Dunlap, fearing that McDowell's entire force was upon him, abandoned Prince's Fort. Hampton's "daring expedition . . . drove back for a time the British and Tory forces, to the happy relief of the people of the surrounding country."[30]

The British faced a number of difficulties in occupying South Carolina. Unless they maintained sufficient troops in a particular neighborhood, local loyalists were subject to reprisals. In an attempt to control the countryside, they established strongholds (such as Prince's Fort) that could serve as bases for patrolling the countryside. Supplying these strongholds soon became a challenge, however, since partisans wasted few opportunities to harass the British.

Hanging Rock and Rocky Mount were the two most important strongholds on the northern frontier. Hanging Rock was east of the Catawba River and almost due north of the courthouse town of Camden. Rocky Mount was about twenty miles away on the western bank of the Catawba. The British supplied these outposts by wagons and packhorses from their base at Camden.

The partisan intelligence network kept various bands informed of British activities. About a week after Huck's Defeat, Major William Richardson Davie of North Carolina was camped near the Waxhaws Church, where he had grown up. A company of South Carolinians, commanded by Major Robert Crawford, soon joined him. In Crawford's company were his teenage brothers-in-law, Andrew and Robert Jackson. Shortly after Davie had established his camp, he received word that the British intended to send a supply convoy to Hanging Rock on 20 July. Like all partisan bands, Davie's was always short of supplies—especially ammunition.[31]

After an all-night march, the North Carolinians established an ambush at Flat Rock, which was about four and a half miles south of Hanging Rock. The wagon train and its Tory militia guards rode right into the trap. Davie's men took what they could use and destroyed the rest. They took their prisoners with them to prevent word of the raid from getting back to Camden.[32]

Concerned about the safety of his party, Davie decided to take a roundabout way back to his camp. But this maneuver did not fool a local Tory unit. About two o'clock the next morning, at Beaver Creek, the partisans were themselves ambushed. In the vanguard of the troop were the Tory prisoners of war, mounted two to a horse and tied together. They presented large targets, and in the exchange of gunfire most of them were killed by their own men. The partisans managed to escape the Tories' snare and made their way back to their camp the next day. It was a close call, but the bottom line was that once again the backcountry partisans had bested the British and their Tory allies. "The object of surprising the convoy was effected," wrote Davie. "The slaughter of the prisoners could not be considered as a loss."[33]

The British had withdrawn from Prince's Fort following the

affair at Earle's Ford and Edward Hampton's daring attack. That left Thicketty Fort in Spartan District as the one remaining British stronghold in the area. It was a formidable log structure with loopholes for firing near the top. Surrounded by a sturdy abatis, it could be entered only by crawling through a small wicket. A few men could easily defend the entrance. During the Regulator troubles of the 1760s, a group of eighty men had successfully held it against more than three hundred outlaws. The fort was in good repair, and the British considered it impregnable except to a cannon barrage.[34]

The fort was commanded by Colonel Patrick Moore, and the garrison included a British sergeant major and some ninety loyalist militia. The Tories stationed at Thicketty Fort regularly essayed out to plunder and terrorize the Whig homesteads for miles around. Many women had been forced to face the enemy alone because their menfolk were either fighting with the partisans or dead. A raiding party from the fort plundered Sarah Steen Jeffries's home and set it afire. They verbally abused her as "the meanest of rebels" and stole all her horses and cattle. After being physically threatened, Nancy Jackson fled her looted home. Moore himself participated in a foray to Samuel McJunkin's farm. After spending the night, the Tories made off with all the family's clothing and all but one of its quilts and blankets.[35]

The McJunkins would have had nothing had not Jane McJunkin challenged a local Tory for possession of her quilt. After the man had placed it on his horse, she ran from the house and snatched it back. The man grabbed the other end, and a tug-of-war ensued. The Tories thought it was great sport, and Moore laughingly decreed that if Jane won the struggle, she could keep her quilt. No one expected this determined Scots-Irish farm woman to best a man in a contest of strength. Then, just as Jane appeared to be losing her grip, the Tory slipped on some fresh, slick horse

manure and went down. Jane McJunkin seized the opportunity
and, placing her foot on the fallen man's chest, gave a mighty
heave—and the quilt came free. To the hoots and cheers of the
Tories, the young woman retreated into her father's house with
her hard-won trophy.[36]

When Sumter learned of these and other "acts of pillaging and
marauding" committed by the garrison at Thicketty Fort, he
decided that something had to be done. He ordered the Georgians to assemble a company of volunteers from his camp and
march on the fort. At Cherokee Ford on the Broad River, the
company met up with McDowell's force, which now numbered
some six hundred men. McDowell and his chief officers, including Andrew Hampton and Isaac Shelby, had already decided to
move against the fort.[37]

With Shelby in command of several hundred men, the partisans set out at sunset on 29 July and arrived at the fort at dawn the
next day. A messenger was sent into the fort under a flag of truce,
calling upon Major Patrick Moore to surrender. Moore responded
that he would defend Thicketty Fort to the last man. Given the
sturdiness of his stronghold and the ample stock of supplies he
had on hand, he could hold out for some time—certainly until
Major Patrick Ferguson, with nearly twice as many men as the
Whigs, came to his rescue.[38]

After Moore refused to surrender, the partisans moved into firing positions all around the fort. After they were in place, a second
ultimatum was sent to the garrison commander. It evidently
included threats of what would happen when—not if—the Whigs
stormed the fort. Knowing that the backcountry partisans meant
business, Moore decided to surrender. Then, after conferring with
his officers, they convinced him to stand firm. He agreed, but
went out to parley with the Whigs. Upon his return to the fort, he
brought back with him "some rebel officers whom he put in pos-

session of the gate and place, who were instantly followed by their men, to the surprise of the garrison."[39]

Once inside, Shelby and his men were amazed to see how fortunate they had been. There were at least two weapons at each loophole, primed and loaded with ball and buckshot. Clearly the Tories could have withstood the siege had their commander showed more backbone. The entire garrison was paroled because McDowell did not want to be burdened with prisoners of war. More than two hundred weapons and ample stocks of powder and shot were welcome prizes of war. Shelby, not knowing the whereabouts of Patrick Ferguson, sent the parolees packing and then hurried his men back to McDowell's camp at Cherokee Ford.[40]

Beginning with Huck's Defeat on 12 July, this action at Thicketty Fort was the seventh consecutive triumph for backcountry partisans over British and Tory troops. The outpost at Thicketty Fort had been captured and that at Prince's Fort abandoned. A detachment of the feared British Legion had been defeated. And at least temporarily, the Tory-induced terror campaign had been suppressed. In the space of thirty days, the patriot cause along the northern frontier had turned 180 degrees. At the end of July 1780, the partisans appeared to have the upper hand in Spartan and New Acquisition Districts.[41]

Given the promising outlook, the various partisan leaders operating in the Catawba River Valley and in the northern districts decided to hold a council of war to plan future operations. Sumter and other South Carolina partisan commanders met with Davie and several other North Carolina officers at Landsford on the Catawba River. They came to an agreement that the two primary British strongholds in the Catawba River Valley, Rocky Mount and Hanging Rock, should be attacked. It was determined that the South Carolinians under Sumter, William Hill, and Edward Lacey would attack Rocky Mount. They would be supported by a detachment of North Carolinians. Simultaneously Davie and another group of North Carolinians would march on Hanging Rock to create a diversion.[42]

Although the leaders had come to a decision, they could not simply order their men into battle. None of them held recognized rank: they had been elected by their men. Thus, they had to explain to their followers what they proposed to do. The plan met with general approval, and each group moved out.

Rocky Mount was aptly named. Three log buildings stood atop a rise beside the Catawba River. The main house had been reinforced to withstand rifle and musket fire. Loopholes provided firing positions for sharpshooters. The camp was surrounded by a ditch with abatis.[43] There were between 150 and 200 members of the New York Volunteers at Rocky Mount under the command of Lieutenant Colonel George Turnbull. Sumter had about 600 men under his command.

On Sunday, 30 July, the partisans deployed around the outpost. Sumter demanded that Turnbull surrender. The British officer replied that "duty and inclination induce me to defend this place to the last extremity." For eight hours there was sporadic firing, and the Whigs "found that we could injure them noways, but by shooting in their portholes." Impatient for results, Sumter ordered a frontal assault that resulted in the death of Colonel Andrew Neel and seven privates.[44]

After a meeting of Sumter's officers, it was decided that the buildings could be set afire. Sumter asked for two volunteers to undertake the hazardous mission. There was silence. No one raised his hand. Then Colonel William Hill stepped forward and said that he would go if another man would accompany him. After another long silence, a second volunteer, a young sergeant, stepped forward.

The men strapped "Rich lightwood" to their bodies and also carried a large bundle of the same material in their arms. There were several large boulders scattered around the property, but they had to cross an open space of one hundred yards. No sooner had they successfully gained cover of one of the boulders than a party from the house charged out with bayonets and chased them back to the partisan lines. A second attempt was made, and with steady fire from the Whig positions occupying the defenders, Hill and his sergeant once again gained the cover of a large boulder. They built a bonfire and began tossing firebrands onto the roof of one of the outbuildings. It caught fire, and the flames threatened to spread to the main house. Then, thinking their mission a success, they ran back to their lines through a hail of gunfire. "I beg leave to remark that Providence so protected us both," wrote Hill, "that neither of us lost a drop of blood, altho' locks of hair was cut from our heads and our garments riddled with balls." Just as it appeared that the main house was blazing up, an afternoon thunderstorm came through and doused the flames. The partisans were forced to withdraw. Casualties on both sides were light, but the British still held Rocky Mount.[45]

During the retreat to Sumter's main camp at Landsford, two of his men were captured by local Tories. Unfortunately, they had originally taken oaths to support the king and had drawn ammunition as Tory militiamen. According to British sources, they had been among a group of Whigs who had taunted the garrison at Rocky Mount with "take back your ammunition again." The British lost no time in proving that they intended to use whatever means were necessary to pacify the state. The prisoners were "hanged as a reward for their treachery."[46]

While Sumter was being thwarted at Rocky Mount, Davie was having great success at Hanging Rock. The plan called for him to make a feint at the stronghold so that the five-hundred-man garrison would concentrate on defending itself and not send any reinforcements to Rocky Mount.

Shortly after noon on 30 July, Davie's small band of about

eighty mounted men approached Hanging Rock. From a local patriot informer they learned that three companies of North Carolina Tories had recently arrived and were in a farmhouse just outside the British lines. Sizing up the situation, Davie divided his troops. He boldly marched half of his men down the road past the farmhouse. Since militia on both sides wore their everyday clothes, not uniforms, it appeared that Davie's men were just some more Tory militia heading toward Hanging Rock. Once these men were in place, Davie stationed twenty dragoons in the road below the house and sent another twenty into an open field beside it.[47]

When the firing started, there was chaos. "The astonished Loyalists fled instantly the other way, and were immediately charged by the dragoons at full gallop and driven back in great confusion," wrote Davie in his memoirs. "[T]hey were surrounded . . . and literally cut to pieces: as this was done under the eye of the whole British camp no prisoners could safely be taken." It was a veritable slaughter. While the British were attempting to form a counterattack from the garrison, Davie's men made off with "sixty valuable Horses with their furniture and one hundred muskets and rifles." There were no Whig casualties. As one modern historian has noted, Davie's action at Hanging Rock "was a textbook model of a partisan operation."[48]

The attacks on Rocky Mount and Hanging Rock were a clear indication that the insurgents had sufficient force and courage to tackle major British troop concentrations. However, Sumter's near-miss at Rocky Mount and Davie's successful raid at Hanging Rock had not dislodged the British. As long as they held these strategic outposts, the Catawba River Valley would not be safe for any Whig. They were challenges that the partisan commanders could not ignore.[49]

Sumter and Davie, with their combined commands of more than eight hundred men, met at Landsford on 5 August to discuss strategy. Determined to strike one of the outposts, they weighed the strengths and weaknesses of each. Although the garrison at Rocky Mount was smaller, its defenses were formidable. There were more British and Tories at Hanging Rock, but they were camped in an open field behind a crude earthen berm. After the leaders agreed that Hanging Rock should be their objective, they consulted with their men, who "entered into the project with great spirit and cheerfulness."[50]

After an all-night march of sixteen miles, the partisans reached the vicinity of the enemy position. Another council of war was held, and there was disagreement between Sumter and Davie as to the plan of attack, but Sumter prevailed. The Whigs divided their force into three columns, each with its own attack sector. The attackers had to negotiate Hanging Rock Creek and a steep ravine in order to reach the camp. It could have been a disaster, but through a misadventure all three Whig columns hit the weakest sector of the British defenses. The Tories defending it were caught totally by surprise, and the enemy's flank was "soon routed with great slaughter."[51]

The partisans fought as if possessed. A detachment of the British Legion mounted a bayonet charge, but they were cut down. Those who survived joined the militia in fleeing the field. At the height of the battle, a Tory regiment slipped into some woods adjacent to the field and began to fire into the Whig lines. The partisans "took instinctively to the trees and bush heaps and returned the fire with deadly effect, in a few minutes there was not a British officer standing, one half the regiment had fallen, and the others on being offered quarters threw down their arms."[52]

Then, with total victory within their grasp, the Whig attack disintegrated. It was the potential for plunder, not British marksmanship, that caused the attack to falter. Despite the urgings of Sumter, Davie, and other officers, almost the entire partisan army stopped fighting and began looting. Clothing, weapons, ammunition, and foodstuffs were taken from tents and wagons. The dead, wounded, and prisoners of war were stripped of anything of value. Several kegs of rum were discovered, and within a short time the men who had responded so coolly under fire three hours earlier were a drunken mob. They ignored the presence of the surviving British and Tories, who had formed a defensive square on the edge of the camp, but were unwilling to renew the battle.[53]

When scouts reported that a British relief force from Rocky Mount was en route, Sumter and Davie managed to get their men to assemble into something resembling a military formation. From their position, the British and Tories gave three cheers for George III, and the partisans answered with three cheers for "the Hero of American Liberty." About one o'clock, the intoxicated partisans moved out in a formation that Davie wryly recorded was not "performed according to the rules of the most approved tactics." It was at Hanging Rock as a messenger for Davie that Andrew Jackson gained his first military experience.[54]

The partisan withdrawal left behind more than two hundred British and Tory killed and wounded. The Prince of Wales Regiment, a regular Tory unit, "was almost annihilated." Of the eight hundred Whigs who entered the battle, twelve were killed and forty-one wounded. The second battle at Hanging Rock was another tremendous patriot victory, but like so many others, it was incomplete. The British still held their outpost—although the scale and success of the partisan assault had greatly shaken the faith of local Tories in the might of British arms.[55]

While Sumter and Davie were operating with impunity along the Catawba, McDowell and his band of nearly one thousand kept on the move in Spartan District. On 8 August, a detachment of partisans under Shelby came into contact with some of Major Patrick Ferguson's men. After an initial stand in which the Whigs repulsed a cavalry charge, the battle became a running fight for three or four miles—from a peach orchard near Cedar Springs to a ford on the Pacolet River. Scouts brought intelligence that Ferguson and his main force of 1,500 to 1,800 men were hot on their trail. Shelby had no intention of letting his band be trapped into a standing engagement and successfully withdrew beyond the Pacolet.[56]

All along the northern frontier, Whig spirits were on the rise. Since Huck's Defeat on 12 July, partisans had reeled off a string of successful actions against the army of occupation and its collaborators. In the swamps of the coastal plain, Francis Marion had assembled a band of intrepid men who would cause the British even more military headaches.

In addition to the partisans' successes, Whig morale was fueled (and Tory resolve undermined) by persistent reports that a large army of Continentals was heading toward South Carolina. The reports were not mere rumors. Congress had selected General Horatio Gates, the hero of the Battle of Saratoga, to command a new southern army. Opinionated, unctuous, and filled with dreams of military glory, Gates was very good at public relations—especially with the Continental Congress, where some considered him a military genius. His campaign in the South, however, was ill fated from the beginning.[57]

Anxious to force a confrontation with Cornwallis, Gates pushed his army mercilessly. The armies on both sides in the Revolution obtained most of their food and forage as they went. Unfortunately for the new southern command (or the "Grand Army," as Gates named it), the route that their commander selected was sparsely settled. Rations were short. Flour and beef, when available, were "so miserably poor that scarce any mortal could make use of it." Officers resorted to thickening their soup with their wig powder. At one point the miserable soldiers came close to mutiny. Totally oblivious to the condition of his men, Gates pressed on.[58]

In central North Carolina, Gates linked up with a small force of Continentals commanded by General Jean DeKalb (often referred to as Baron DeKalb). DeKalb, who had been in the Carolinas for several months and had a solid grasp of what was going on, counseled marching west to the Catawba River Valley in North Carolina, then heading south toward Camden. In this way, the army could take advantage of the partisan-controlled region that stretched from west and north of Camden in South Carolina to Salisbury in North Carolina. Gates ignored DeKalb's suggestions and those of other officers and ordered the army to take the most direct route possible for Camden. The pine and turkey oak barrens through which the army marched yielded nothing in the way of supplies. A nineteenth-century historian wrote that the region "nearly resembled a desert."[59]

Partisans now came forward to meet with the American commander. Despite the obvious success of Tarleton and the various partisans, Gates considered mounted troops useless in the South. He had little regard for the partisans and was particularly contemptuous of Francis Marion and his band. Fortunately for South Carolina and the United States, Gates ordered Marion to leave his camp and move into the coastal region to observe and harass the enemy.[60]

The one person Gates paid any attention to was Thomas Sumter. Perhaps it was because the Gamecock, as he was now affectionately called by his men, styled himself as a general. Perhaps it was because of Sumter's successes in the field (although Davie, McDowell, and Shelby had been just as successful). Or perhaps Gates and the Gamecock were equally vain and impetuous. Whatever the reason, Gates disregarded the advice of his own officers and listened to Sumter's.

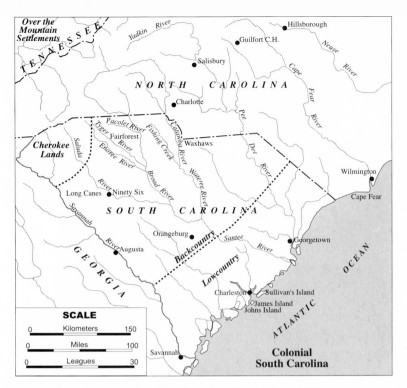

Colonial South Carolina. Based on Kovacick and Winberry,
South Carolina: The Making of a Landscape.

South Carolina Election Districts, 1776. Based on Edgar,
South Carolina: A History.

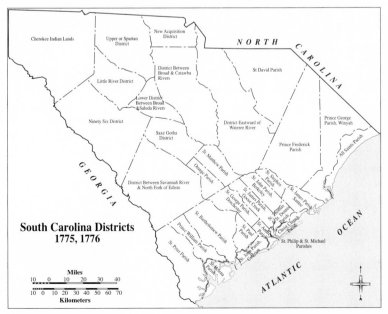

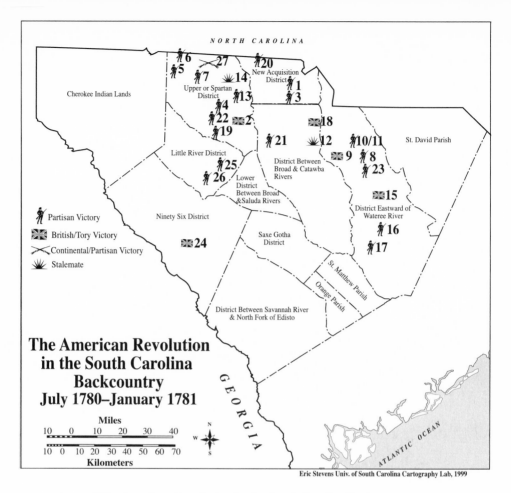

The American Revolution in the South Carolina Backcountry,
July 1780–January 1781.

1. Huck's Defeat	10. Hanging Rock	19. Musgrove's Mill
2. Brandon's Defeat	11. Hanging Rock	20. King's Mountain
3. Stallions	12. Rocky Mount	21. Fishdam Ford
4. Cedar Springs	13. Thicketty Fort	22. Blackstock's
5. Gowen's Old Fort	14. Old Iron Works	23. Ruguley's Mills
6. Earle's Ford	15. Camden	24. Long Cane
7. Prince's Fort	16. Wateree Ferry	25. Hammond's Store
8. Flat Rock	17. Convoy From Ninety Six	26. William's Fort
9. Beaver Creek	18. Fishing Creek	27. Cowpens

The Lawrence Corley Cabin (built circa 1771), Saxe Gotha District,
was typical of dwellings in the South Carolina backcountry.

"Liberty or Death," a fireback cast at William Hill's Aero Furnace,
New Acquisition District.

Banastre Tarleton, "Bloody Tarleton."

MAJ GEN THOMAS SUMTER

Thomas Sumter.

The Battle of King's Mountain. Note in the center of the drawing,
Patrick Ferguson's riderless white horse and his body slightly behind it.

The Battle of King's Mountain. By Eric Stevens, University of South Carolina
Cartography Lab, 1999. Based on McCrady, *The History of South Carolina in the Revolution,
1775–1780*, and Wickwire and Wickwire, *Cornwallis.*

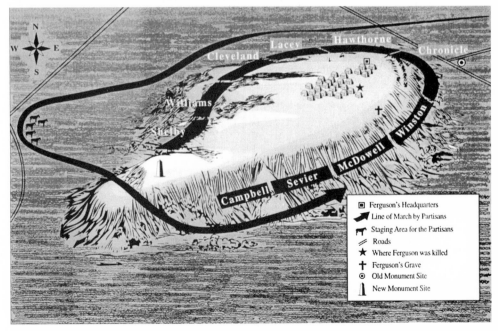

A member of the British Legion threatened to kill Martha Bratton unless
she revealed the whereabouts of local partisans. Original from *Harper's Weekly*.

As Gates's army neared South Carolina, the British pulled back their garrisons from Rocky Mount and Hanging Rock. Cornwallis intended to concentrate his forces at Camden. Sumter proposed to Gates that Sumter's planned attack on Camden would be helped immeasurably if Gates were to detach men to assist him in raiding the British line of communications between Camden and Charleston. Although a major battle was in the offing there, Gates somehow saw merit in Sumter's proposal and gave him what he asked for.[61]

Sumter wasted little time in implementing his plan. This time he hit a small outpost on the Wateree River below Camden. A garrison of thirty men defended a makeshift fort at a ferry crossing—a vital link in the British communications chain. A detachment of Sumter's band commanded by Colonel Thomas Taylor took the outpost by surprise and captured the entire garrison and thirty-six wagons full of war matériel. In questioning his prisoners, Taylor discovered that a wagon convoy was en route from Ninety Six. Taking advantage of this intelligence, the resourceful Taylor planned and executed a successful ambush.[62]

Sumter informed Gates of the capture of the crucial ferry crossing and said that he would defend it until he received instructions to the contrary. No sooner had his report gone out than the British began crossing the Wateree in large numbers below the ferry. Without hesitation, Sumter withdrew his men and moved his command ten miles up the river. According to his biographer, the Gamecock was more interested in protecting his plunder than in the general military situation.[63]

Gates, anxious to win more laurels for himself, had pushed his army to the point of exhaustion. On 15 August, Cornwallis moved out from Camden with Gates's army as his objective. Almost simultaneously, Gates ordered his army forward to seek out the British. The Americans were ill prepared for battle. Besides being physically worn out from forced marches, their evening rations on 14 August had caused them nothing but misery. Because of Gates's haste to engage the enemy, the meat was only partially cooked and a dessert of molasses and corn mush caused diarrhea. According to contemporary accounts, the Americans "were breaking ranks all night and were certainly much debilitated before action commenced in the morning."[64]

Early on the morning of the sixteenth, the advance parties met. Although the Americans outnumbered the British three thousand to two thousand, only nine hundred of Gates's command were Continentals; the remainder were Virginia and North Carolina militia. Nearly 70 percent of the British army were either British or Tory regulars; the rest were North Carolina militia.[65]

As the two armies maneuvered for battle, Gates made one military gaffe after another. He assigned unseasoned militia troops to cover the American left and a portion of the regulars to the right. He kept the remainder of his Continentals in reserve. It was no contest. At the first sight of the British advancing with fixed bayonets, the militia broke and ran. Some accounts said they threw down their loaded weapons and never fired a shot. The Continentals under DeKalb stood their ground. Twice they turned back the British, but eventually they were overwhelmed. The brave DeKalb suffered eight bayonet and three bullet wounds. Three days later he died.[66]

General Gates did not stick around to see the final outcome of the battle. He mounted his horse and did not stop until he reached Charlotte, North Carolina, about 70 miles away. He then procured a fresh horse and galloped off another 120 miles to Hillsboro—to put as much distance as he could between himself and Cornwallis's victorious army.[67]

The vanquished Whigs—those who were able—fled north toward Charlotte. Tarleton and his legion relentlessly pursued the remnants of Gates's army. Charles Stedman, a Tory officer, reported the aftermath of the battle. "The road for some miles was strewed with the wounded and killed, who had been overtaken by the legion in their pursuit. The number of dead horses, broken waggons, and baggage, scattered on the road, formed a perfect sense of terror and confusion: arms, knapsacks and accoutrements found were innumerable: such was the terror and dismay of the Americans." The description brings to mind the Iraqi retreat from Kuwait in 1991 during Operation Desert Storm.[68]

If ever there was a military disaster, the Battle of Camden was one. Of the 3,000-plus members of Gates's southern army who entered the battle, only about 700 regrouped at Hillsboro. Estimates of the number of killed range from 250 to 800; between 900 and 1,000 men were wounded and taken prisoner. The rest of the army simply vanished. All of the American artillery and almost all of its ammunition and supply wagons were captured.[69]

Sumter, unaware of the outcome at Camden, had been moving north at a leisurely rate along the western bank of the Catawba. On the evening of 16 August, messengers dispatched by Davie reached the partisan camp. The alarming news did cause Sumter to increase his pace, but his column could not move as fast as he would have liked. Had he had only his men, he could have disappeared into the countryside. However, some fifty wagons of captured war matériel and 250 prisoners of war were slowing him down. Cornwallis wanted to recover both the men and the munitions, and he wanted to punish Thomas Sumter. He gave Banastre Tarleton and the British Legion the mission.[70]

Tarleton immediately set out up the east bank of the Catawba. The day after the battle at Camden, Sumter had moved only as far as Rocky Mount. On the evening of 17 August, Sumter bivouacked out in the open along the riverbank. His men built fires to prepare their evening meal. From the other side of the river, Tarleton could easily spot the partisan camp. To keep from revealing his position, Tarleton ordered his men not to build fires. After Sumter moved out the next morning, the British crossed the river in boats and gave chase.[71]

It was a stifling August day in the Catawba River Valley. The humidity at that time of the year hovers in the 80 to 90 percent range. At noon, after an eight-mile march under difficult conditions, Sumter halted at the banks of Fishing Creek, a major tributary of the Catawba. Despite the warnings he had received, he took no special security precautions. There were a few sentries along the road, but most men were using the halt in the march for rest and recreation. They stacked arms and relaxed. Many took the opportunity to swim and bathe in the creek. Others, including their commander, decided to take a nap in whatever shade they could find.[72]

With his usual impetuosity, skill, and luck, Tarleton advanced on the partisan camp. His foot soldiers were exhausted, but he had his legionnaires and mounted infantry. "The decision, and preparation for the attack, were momentary," wrote Tarleton in his memoirs. "The cavalry and [mounted] infantry formed into one line, and, giving a general shout, advanced to the charge." It was no contest. The Whigs, many caught quite literally with their pants down, were routed. Sumter, asleep under a wagon, awoke as the green-coated legionnaires swept into the camp. Unable to get to his mount, he cut the harness of a draft horse from a wagon and tried to rally his men. It was not possible, and the semi-clad Gamecock fled into the nearby woods.[73]

The disaster at Camden was followed by the fiasco at Fishing Creek. Tarleton accomplished his mission. He recovered the munitions and freed the prisoners of war. He captured all of Sumter's supply train, 800 horses, 1,000 individual weapons, and his artillery. The British lost only 16 men killed or wounded. The

American losses were severe: 150 men killed or wounded and more than 300 prisoners of war. Among the casualties and POWs were the Continentals whom Gates had sent to support Sumter's operations. Several days later, Sumter had made his way to Davie's band in Charlotte, where, in the words of a biographer, he was "a brigadier general without servant, soldier, or vestige of a brigade."[74]

Cornwallis was jubilant. After a succession of partisan victories, the British army had defeated a second Continental army in South Carolina and the pesky Sumter had been routed. When news of these triumphs reached London, the earl was the toast of the capital. When the Comte de Vergennes, Louis XVI's foreign minister, learned of the defeats at Camden and Fishing Creek, he believed that the American cause was lost. He floated a peace feeler based upon *uti possidetis* ("as you possess") that would have left South Carolina and Georgia as British colonies. "Notwithstanding the commotions had been violent, and almost general, in South Carolina," wrote Tarleton, "it was imagined and hoped that these internal troubles would subside, when the inhabitants gained information of the late distinguished superiority which had attended His Majesty's arms." Cornwallis was not as confident as his subordinate, but he, too, hoped that "the internal commotions and insurrections in the province will now subside."[75]

Lord Cornwallis was convinced that North Carolina was the key to holding South Carolina. As long as Gates and the tattered remnants of his army remained at Hillsboro, they provided the partisans in South Carolina with hope. "[I]f we do not attack that province," he wrote, "we must give up both South Carolina and Georgia, and retire within the walls of Charleston." He was therefore determined to move his army across the border.[76]

Although their commander may have insisted that they push into North Carolina, the troops of Cornwallis's command were in

no condition to do so. Exhausted by the unrelenting South Carolina heat and humidity and weakened by a variety of fevers, the
British remained in the vicinity of Camden for several weeks.
They did begin their march on 8 September, but they went no
more than twenty miles or so before they stopped to rest for
another two weeks.[77]

For several weeks after Camden and Fishing Creek, there
was little military activity in the Catawba River Valley. However,
the day after Sumter's defeat at Fishing Creek, there was a significant engagement on the border between Spartan and Little
River Districts.

On 18 August, a party of two hundred mounted partisans left
McDowell's Camp in Spartan District and headed out to raid a
Tory outpost at Musgrove's Mill. The men rode all night, and
early the next day their scouts ran into some loyalist scouts. Shots
were exchanged, and both parties retreated. Then a friendly
farmer informed the Whig commanders that instead of a small garrison of local Tories, the enemy numbered about five hundred, of
whom two hundred were Tory regulars. With their attack compro-
mised and their horses worn out, the partisans decided to go on
the defensive. Within a short period of time, they created a semi-
circular breastwork of logs and brush on a ridge above the Enoree
River.

A party of twenty or so mounted men volunteered to cross the
river, engage the enemy, and draw them into the ambush. The
mixed patriot militia (South Carolinians, Georgians, and "Over
Mountain Men" from present-day Tennessee) held their fire
until the attackers were within about seventy yards of their position. Then they opened up with devastating effect. At one point
it looked as if Tory regulars would turn the partisans' right flank,
but screaming Over Mountain Men rushed into the fray. As the
British lines wavered and then broke, the Whigs leaped from

their defensive positions "yelling, shooting, and slashing on every hand."[78]

Within an hour, it was over. Of the 500 British and loyalists who had charged the Whig defenses, 153 were killed or wounded and 70 taken prisoner. The victorious partisans were considering following up their success by heading toward Ninety Six when they received word of Gates's defeat at Camden. Realizing that they were the only American force in the upper part of the state, they opted to retreat into North Carolina. With one of Patrick Ferguson's patrols dogging them most of the way, the partisans did not stop to rest or eat as they made good their escape. After they reached a safe haven in western North Carolina, the Over Mountain Men returned home, but the various commanders agreed to keep one another informed of Ferguson's activities.[79]

As Cornwallis marched on Charlotte, Ferguson and about one thousand loyalist militia headed for western North Carolina. Behind them they left a very unpacified South Carolina. Within two weeks after his defeat at Fishing Creek, Sumter had raised another partisan force of nearly one thousand. On 29 August, Cornwallis wrote General Clinton in New York that "the indefatigable Sumter is again in the field, and is beating up for recruits with the greatest assiduity." Two days later, Gates wrote General Washington that the Gamecock had "reinstated and increased his corps to upwards of 1,000 men" and that he had ordered him "to continue to harass the enemy." Sumter did not do much to bedevil the enemy over the next six weeks, but Francis Marion did. From his lairs in the Pee Dee swamps, the Swamp Fox terrorized Tories, attacked isolated outposts, and raided British supply convoys.[80]

The sections of North Carolina where the British were headed were just as inhospitable as South Carolina. The town of Charlotte and surrounding Mecklenburg County were in the upper reaches of the Catawba River Valley. Cornwallis occupied Charlotte, but partisans under Davie and others made life miserable for British patrols and convoys.[81]

Meanwhile, as Ferguson marched into the western frontier settlements he sent a personal message to Colonel Isaac Shelby. If the residents of the region "did not desist from their opposition to British arms, he would march his army over the mountains, hang their leaders, and lay their country waste with fire and sword." Shelby did not hesitate once he had received the message from his cousin, who had been a British prisoner. He contacted other leading men in the Over Mountain settlements and a call went out to meet on 25 September on the banks of the Watauga River in present-day Tennessee. About one thousand frontiersmen, many armed with rifles, showed up on the appointed day. A local Presbyterian clergyman, the Reverend Samuel Doak, preached a sermon based upon Gideon's successful uprising against the Midianites. Like the Reverend John Simpson and the Reverend William Martin, Doak assured his listeners that they were fighting with the Lord God Jehovah on their side. Their battle cry should be, he roared: "The sword of the Lord and of Gideon!"[82]

The "backwoods plunderers," as Ferguson had termed them, crossed the mountains into western North Carolina. Just as Cornwallis was moving toward Charlotte, Ferguson received intelligence that a large patriot force was on the march and that he was its target. Despite this news, on 1 October, he issued a proclamation that further infuriated both the Over Mountain Men and local patriots. After reciting a tale of partisan atrocities (which may well have been true), he said that if the men of North Carolina "wish or desire to live, and bear the name of men, grasp your arms in a moment and run to camp. . . . If you choose to be degraded forever and ever by a set of mongrels, say so at once, and let your women turn their backs upon you, and look out for real men to protect them."[83]

Ferguson's proclamation was an act of false bravado. No sooner had he issued it than he began to retreat toward Charlotte. During the first week in October, partisan bands from the two Carolinas and Georgia joined the Over Mountain Men. On 6 October, they camped at Saunders' Cowpens in Spartan District. Among them were William Hill, James Williams, Edward Lacey, Edward Hampton, and Joseph Kerr. Kerr, because of his physical handicap, had once again been able to spy on the enemy without arousing suspicion. He had been with Ferguson earlier in the day and brought word that the enemy was going to bivouac at King's Mountain.[84]

The exact number of partisans tracking Ferguson has never been determined. Most estimates give the combined total of the several groups at between nine hundred and eleven hundred. There was no organized Whig command. As usual, the various group leaders met in a council of war to discuss strategy. They chose as their commander William Campbell, one of the Over Mountain Men. They decided to send nine hundred mounted men to seek out Ferguson, and those on foot would follow.[85]

Within twenty-four hours, they confirmed the intelligence that Kerr had brought them. Ferguson was indeed on King's Mountain, but he was doing more than just setting up a camp. He had decided to make a stand even though he knew the odds were not in his favor. In a message to Cornwallis, he wrote: "[I]f necessary, I should hope for success against them myself; but numbers compared, that must be doubtful. I am on my march towards you by a road leading from Cherokee ford, north of King's Mountain." He was only about thirty miles from Cornwallis's main body at Charlotte and, given the mobility of his eleven-hundred-man force, probably could have reached there safely. Perhaps it was British arrogance and contempt for the locals that caused him to decide to confront his enemies.[86]

King's Mountain, the site he chose to defend, is not really a mountain but one of the highest ridges in a series of ridges that runs along the border of the two Carolinas. It rises 60 feet above the surrounding countryside. At its base, it is 600 yards long and 250 yards wide, but at its peak only 60 yards by 120 yards. In 1780 the mountain's steep, rocky slopes were covered with trees that would have provided cover for backcountry marksmen. The overconfident Ferguson did not construct any defensive positions. "I arrived today at King's Mountain & have taken a post where I do not think I can be forced by a stronger enemy than that against us."[87]

It began raining on 7 October and continued until midday on the eighth. Another council of war produced a simple battle plan. The partisans would form ranks two men deep on three sides of the mountain and attack. Late in the afternoon the battle began. Colonel Campbell stepped forward and bellowed: "Here they are, my brave boys; *shout like Hell, and fight like devils!*" The Whigs needed little encouragement. They had their enemy trapped. Shelby's men fired the first shots as the Whigs advanced.[88]

On the mountain, the defenders fixed their bayonets and charged the advancing troops. There were at least two, perhaps three, bayonet charges. All of them were repulsed. The defenders, firing downhill, shot over the heads of their attackers. From behind rocks and trees, the frontiersmen—almost all armed with rifles—picked off the Tories as if it were a turkey shoot. On the mountaintop, it was chaos. With fire coming in from every side and with their ammunition running low, many Tories were ready to quit. Several had already raised flags of surrender.[89]

Ferguson made one last attempt to turn the tide of battle. In a last desperate effort to break through Whig lines, he rallied a small group around him. "Huzza, brave boys," he shouted, "the day is our own." Then, on his white steed, he led a charge down the mountain. He was cut down before he got twenty yards. According to James Collins, a young Whig, "[s]even rifle balls had passed through his body, both his arms were broken and his hat and clothing literally shot to pieces."[90]

Seeing that the battle was lost, several Tory officers tried to surrender and asked for quarter. "Give them Buford's play!" was the response from many a revenge-minded Whig. On the second attempt, the surrender of what was left of Ferguson's force was successful. It was with great difficulty that Shelby, Campbell, and other officers restrained their men.[91]

What happened afterward is subject to dispute, but there is little doubt that the victorious partisans treated their conquered foes as they and their neighbors had been treated. The body of the fallen British commander was stripped and left naked where he had died. Any item that was identified as his possession became a highly sought war trophy. Tarleton, in his memoirs, wrote that "[t]he mountaineers . . . used every insult and indignity . . . towards the dead body of Major Ferguson." There were rumors that a number of Over Mountain Men, in a frontier show of contempt, undid their breeches and pissed on Ferguson's corpse.[92]

In less than an hour, the partisans had destroyed a superior force of more than 1,000 provincial regulars and Tory militia. Besides Ferguson, there were 156 dead. Some 163 Tories were wounded, and another 698 were taken prisoner. The victorious Whigs lost fewer than 100 men (28 killed, 62 wounded).[93]

As the prisoners were being rounded up, a Tory foraging party returned to the scene of the battle. Not realizing what had occurred, they opened fire on the Whigs and mortally wounded Colonel James Williams. The partisans, fearful that either the

POWs were trying to mutiny or that Tarleton's advance party was upon them, opened fire on the unarmed prisoners.[94]

Unsure of what Cornwallis, only thirty miles away, might do, the Over Mountain Men were anxious to head back to western North Carolina. There was little time or sympathy for their defeated foes. On the field of battle lay a wounded Tory. He saw his brother-in-law, a partisan captain, and pleaded for succor. "Look to your friends for help" was the cold reply. That brief exchange clearly revealed the depths of the bitter feelings on both sides of what was America's first civil war. Those feelings were exhibited again several days later after the Whigs had withdrawn to the mountains. At the insistence of partisans from the two Carolinas, a trial was held. Thirty-six Tories were condemned to death for various atrocities against their neighbors, but only nine were hanged.[95]

One British account of the affair, after congratulating the partisans on their "brilliant" victory, said that "they shamefully stained the laurels they had won by cruelties exercised upon the prisoners, ten of whom were hanged immediately after the action." Yet the same observer had justified the hanging of Whig prisoners who took protection from the British and then joined the enemy. "Instant death" was pronounced on those unfortunates who fell into British hands because it was thought that "the terrors of punishment" would dissuade others. For South Carolina partisans who had seen their captured comrades hanged at Camden and Ninety Six, it was simple frontier justice, not cruelty. In a burst of incredible hypocrisy, Tarleton condemned the actions of the partisans who, he wrote, "exercised horrid cruelties on the prisoners that fell into their possession."[96]

Since the 1760s, backcountry settlers had been fighting one another, the Cherokee, and the British. It was a struggle for survival, and the niceties of "civilized warfare" were ignored. In their attempts to pacify South Carolina, Tarleton, Wemyss, and even Cornwallis behaved in ways that triggered savage reprisals. "Grim and relentless" was the way one modern military historian characterized the fighting in the South Carolina backcountry. In America's first civil war, there were no holds barred. It was a conflict in which "the virtue of humanity was totally forgot."[97]

6

"No Quarter!": The Desperate Struggle in the South Carolina Backcountry

*The Whigs and Tories pursue one another with the most relentless
fury, killing and destroying each other whenever they meet. . . .
The great bodies of militia that have been in service this year . . .
have laid waste the country. . . .*
NATHANAEL GREENE, DECEMBER 1780

For two decades, the South Carolina backcountry had been
in turmoil. Violence and anarchy had been more common
than peace and stability. The Cherokee War and its aftermath had led to the Regulator movement of the late 1760s. In
subduing the Cherokee, the frontier militia had done what they
could to destroy the Cherokee nation. They had practiced a
scorched-earth policy against the Indians: burning villages, killing
cattle, destroying orchards and fields. The struggle between the
bandits and the law-abiding settlers (who would become the Regulators) was a preview of the Revolution in the backcountry. Tor-

ture, murder, and arson were considered acceptable means of dealing with one's foes. When the state started down the road toward revolution, a sizable number of those who had been Regulators opted to fight for independence. And a good many backcountry residents who had opposed the Regulators supported the king's cause.

As early as the fall and winter of 1775–76, the actions of those on both sides in the backcountry had taken a nasty turn. The complaints of the British about the treatment of prisoners of war after the battle at King's Mountain rang hollow. Although the regular British military establishment had not initiated the brutal, reprisal- and revenge-driven conflict in the South Carolina backcountry, it can be argued that it was the conduct of the British army of occupation that caused the savagery to descend to lower levels.

In August 1780, Cornwallis wrote to Lieutenant Colonel John Harris Cruger, the commander at Ninety Six. He gave orders that all inhabitants of South Carolina who had taken the king's protection and then participated in the new uprisings "should be punished with the greatest rigour." They should be imprisoned and their property either confiscated or destroyed. Tories who had suffered property losses at the hands of Whig partisans could be compensated with appropriated Whig property. Any "militia man who had borne arms with us and had afterwards joined the enemy should be immediately hanged." The commander of the army of occupation then directed that his subordinate "take the most *vigorous* measures to *extinguish the rebellion* in the district you command, and that you will obey in the strictest manner the directions I have given in this letter, relative to the treatment of the country."[1]

Although Cornwallis had defeated Gates at Camden, the partisans were still attacking convoys, intimidating loyalists, and harassing patrols. The British general finally realized the nature of the conflict in which he found himself. "[I]n a civil war," he wrote

Cruger, "there is no admitting of neutral characters, & those who are not clearly with us must be so far considered against us, as to be disarmed, and *every measure taken to prevent their being able to do mischief.*" "Every measure taken" was interpreted quite literally by Wemyss, Tarleton, Ferguson, and other subordinates.[2]

On the American side, Nathanael Greene, a hardened veteran who would later command the Continental army in South Carolina, was stunned at the "growing enormities" occurring in the backcountry. One of his aides blamed the situation on the enemy: "For want of civil government the bands of society are totally disunited, and the people, by copying the manners of the British, have become perfectly savage."[3]

Since violence was endemic to the frontier, some observers might think it unfair to place the blame for the barbaric nature of the warfare in South Carolina on the British. However, even historians of South Carolina's loyalists concur that a brutal civil war erupted after the British capture of Charleston and the occupation of the backcountry.[4]

The British, in trying to pacify the populace, made one mistake after another. British hauteur and contempt did not serve Cornwallis and his officers well in trying to understand the situation. Although Cornwallis wrote that he knew that the British were involved in a civil war, the conduct of the army of occupation undermined any real hope of pacification.

One of the major difficulties was trying to figure out who was on whose side. In William Gilmore Simms's *The Scout*, one character comments that it is difficult to trust even your brother. "A man's best friend now-a-days is . . . his rifle. You may call his jack-knife a first cousin, and his two pistols his eldest sons; and even then, there's no telling which of them all is going to fail him first, or whether any one among 'em will stick by him till the scratch is over." Some weapons, like kinfolk, might betray you at a crucial moment. Had Edward Lacey not tied his father to his bedstead, the old man intended to provide Captain Huck with information that probably would have resulted in his son's capture or death. Captain Love buried his Tory sister killed in the fight at Stallions. And a partisan captain ignored the pleas of his dying brother-in-law on the field at King's Mountain.[5]

By some accounts, individuals might have switched sides as many as four or five times. To the British, anyone who had taken the king's protection and then joined a partisan band was guilty of treason. After the Battle of Camden, Cornwallis decreed "Instant death" on those prisoners of war who had changed sides. Charles Stedman, one of his staff, wrote that hanging turncoats had become "necessary to restrain their perfidy by examples of severity, and the terrors of punishment." But such a draconian measure did not intimidate as much as it infuriated backcountry residents.[6]

The British also looted and pillaged at will. Prior to August 1780, Tories and Whigs already had done their share of ransacking one another's farms. Tarleton wrote Cornwallis that "many of the insurgents having taken certificates & paroles don't deserve leniency. None shall they experience. I have promised the young men who chuse to assist me in this expedition the plunder of the leaders of the faction." However, Cornwallis's instructions legitimized theft and, along with "Tarleton's quarter" and Cornwallis's hanging of prisoners of war, led to reprisals.[7]

Not only deaths were avenged, but thefts and property confiscations as well. Sumter's band was notorious for its desire for booty. As a recruiting device, the Gamecock offered a payment of a specified number of slaves per year depending on an individual's rank. A private received one slave for signing up for a ten-month hitch, while a major got three for a year's enlistment. Some officers, such as Wade Hampton, were disgusted with the conduct of some of their fellow partisans, who "combined in committing robberies, the most base and inhuman that ever disgraced mankind." The civil war in the backcountry was not just an eye for an eye and a tooth for a tooth; it was also a "horse for a horse, even a Negro for a Negro."[8]

Revenge was a major factor in motivating participants on both sides. The Tory Thomas "Burnfoot" Brown showed no mercy to partisans because of the torture he had suffered very early in the Revolution. Thomas Sumter resumed his fight against the British after Tarleton burned his plantation. And the same held true for many of the Scots-Irish in the Catawba River Valley. Although William "Bloody Bill" Cunningham was a loyalist sympathizer, he did not begin his notorious rampages in Ninety Six District until after the 1778 murder of his crippled, epileptic brother by partisan raiders. Almost all of Cunningham's men had been driven from their homes; many had been in exile in Florida. In particular, loyalists sought retribution once the British army entered South Carolina.[9]

The conduct of individuals and the various partisan bands was often shaped by experience. For example, when several of Francis Marion's scouts stopped at a farmhouse for food and were surprised by a large party of Tories, they surrendered after they were promised quarter. As soon as they were taken into custody, however, the Tories "butchered them in cold blood." After that incident, Marion's men went into battle with the cry "No quarter for Tories." They and other partisans did, however, treat British regulars as prisoners of war.[10]

When Sumter captured the hated James Wemyss in November 1780, the British officer feared for his life. For in his possession he had a detailed list of the partisans he had executed and the homesteads he had destroyed. Sumter read the list and casually threw it into a fire. Had Sumter's men discovered the list, the Gamecock would have not been able to prevent them from stringing up

Wemyss from the nearest tree. In this instance, a partisan's gallantry saved the life of a wounded British officer. One wonders what Sumter would have done if he had known that Wemyss had sent a special assassination team after him.[11]

Among the many frustrations the British experienced throughout their occupation of South Carolina was the lack of leadership among the local Tories. With the exceptions of Thomas Brown, Thomas Fletchell, William Cunningham, and the Reverend Philip Mulkey, they did not attract many of the leading men of the backcountry to their cause. And with the exception of Brown, those who did espouse the king's cause were not of the same caliber as their counterparts fighting in the various partisan bands.[12]

Mulkey was a powerful preacher and influential member of the Fairforest community, and Thomas Fletchell agreed with his minister on supporting the king's cause. However, Mulkey could not convince a majority of his Fairforest Baptist congregation to follow him into the Tory camp. In contrast, William Martin and John Simpson not only persuaded their congregations to fight the British but became actively involved in the conflict themselves. Martin's incarceration by the British became a symbol of their tyranny. Simpson not only urged his flock to resist but joined Sumter's partisan band and participated in a number of engagements, including Fishing Creek. These Presbyterian clergy were among the leading men of the backcountry even before the Revolution had "been laying deep their fatal Republican Notions and Principles—Especially—That they owe no subjugation to Great Britain—That they are a free People."[13]

Within a few months of fighting the partisans in the backcountry, the British decided that if they could not recruit leaders on principle, then they would buy them. Cornwallis is supposed to have met with Richard Richardson, one of the most respected men in the backcountry. He offered the elderly man "any office or title he might wish" if he would only agree to support the king's cause. If he did not—and there was a stick with the carrot—then he would be imprisoned. The seventy-six-year-old former militia general did not hesitate. "I have from the best convictions of my mind," he told Cornwallis, "embarked in a cause which I think righteous and just; I have knowingly staked my life, family, and property all upon the issue. I am prepared to suffer or triumph with it, and would rather die a thousand deaths than betray my country or deceive my friends." As a consequence of his resolve, he was jailed. Richardson became seriously ill and was sent home, where, under house arrest, he died in September 1780.[14]

Edward Lacey did not have a great deal of personal wealth, and what little he did have was either stolen or destroyed in several Tory raids on his farm. Despite his youth and lack of wealth, he was a born military leader and highly respected by his neighbors. At some point in 1780, the British offered him a sizable amount of gold to join their Tory militia. His loyalty, like Richard Richardson's, could not be suborned.[15]

If partisan leaders could not be persuaded or bought, then perhaps they could be eliminated. The British offered a reward of 500 guineas ($25,000) to anyone who would lead them to Thomas Sumter.[16]

On 7 November 1780, a Tory named Sealy came to Cornwallis's headquarters at Winnsboro with the news that he knew where Sumter was camped. Earlier that morning he had been stopped by a partisan scouting party and taken into custody. He had convinced his questioners and Sumter that he was a good Whig and was released. Then he wasted no time in hightailing it to the British. Major James Wemyss was the first officer to whom he told his story. Wemyss, in turn, rushed to Cornwallis with a plan to take out Sumter and his band. The opportunity of "defeating so daring and troublesome a man as Sumpter [*sic*], and dispersing such a banditti," noted Cornwallis, "was a great object." He gave Wemyss permission to lead a raid against the partisans' camp on the Broad River.[17]

With a party of forty members of Tarleton's legion and one hundred mounted infantry, Wemyss set out. Sumter was not where Sealy thought he would be; he had moved his camp about five miles to Fishdam Ford on the east bank of the Broad River. Wemyss made better time than he had anticipated, and shortly after midnight on 9 November he ran into Sumter's outlying pickets. They fired into the British, wounding Wemyss and knocking him out of the battle. His subordinates led a charge into the partisans' camp across open ground. Silhouetted against the campfires, the British were easy targets. Their initial foray was blunted, as was a dismounted bayonet charge.[18]

While the battle was raging, Sealy and a party of five dragoons from Tarleton's legion were to head for Sumter's tent and either kill or capture him. For some reason, Sumter was still asleep as the battle developed. He was trying to get dressed when he heard running feet near his tent. Sensing danger, he threw himself out of the back of his tent as two dragoons entered it. Barefoot and dressed only in his underwear, the partisan commander fled for his life. He jumped over a fence, ran through a briar patch, and plunged down the riverbank. For most of the night he huddled at the edge of the river until the British were driven back. Later Sumter recalled that "it was with the greatest difficulty that I escaped being cut to pieces."[19]

In the melee, Sealy was one of four British and Tories killed in action. Wemyss was one of some twenty wounded who fell into Sumter's hands. Cornwallis was furious at the botched raid and shortly sent Tarleton out after Sumter. At the Battle of Blackstock's in Spartan District eleven days later, Sumter defeated Tarleton (although in his reports to Cornwallis, Tarleton lied about the results). Tarleton lost ninety-two killed and seventy-six wounded while the Whig losses were light, only three killed and four wounded. However, among the wounded was Thomas Sumter.[20]

The next day Tarleton sent a party out after the retreating partisans. In his correspondence, he was preoccupied with dispatching the Gamecock. He wrote to Cornwallis that "three young men of Ferguson's Corps have promised to fix Sumter immediately." To encourage the men in their enterprise, he promised them 50 guineas ($2,500) "for the deed." For two days Tarleton's scouts hotly pursued Sumter and his small party. Eventually they broke off the chase, and the severely wounded Gamecock, confined to a rude litter, was carried to a place of safety in New Acquisition District. Cornwallis, hoping for the best, wrote Tarleton that he would "be very glad to hear that Sumter is in a condition to give us no further trouble; he certainly has been our greatest plague in this country."[21]

But it was not to be. Not that Tarleton did not try to put Sumter permanently out of commission. Tarleton had met his first defeat at Blackstock's, and his fury turned personal. Like Wemyss, he was willing to do whatever was necessary to eliminate Thomas Sumter. Both British officers resorted to assassination teams and promises of financial reward to try to accomplish by covert means what they could not accomplish on the battlefield.

Given the actions of Tarleton and Wemyss, it is ironic that the British protested the "uncivilized" actions of their foes. They accused the partisans of murdering prisoners of war, but unashamedly did the same. In 1781, Thomas Sumter seized a British convoy near the Santee River. According to British accounts, after the British had laid down their arms, a party of Sumter's cavalry "who said they had not discharged their pieces came up, fired upon the prisoners and killed seven of them." Several days later, a British patrol captured six of Sumter's men. "Enquire," cryptically commented a British officer, "how they were treated."[22]

Lord Cornwallis, outraged by the partisans' brutal treatment of loyalists, vowed to "retaliate on the unfortunate persons" in his custody. Yet, after Camden, he had already done so. Not only had he ordered "perfidious" prisoners hanged, but he had personally witnessed their execution. Cornwallis did little to curb his officers such as Tarleton, Wemyss, and Ferguson. He did, however, occasionally discipline Tories. Because of Burnfoot Brown's habit of using torture, Cornwallis ordered him out of South Carolina and into Georgia, where he continued his old ways.[23]

In the 1990s, incidents of terrorism and brutality are regular features on the evening news. As a society, we have become somewhat inured to the violence all around us. Yet across the distance of two centuries, the level of brutality and cruelty that Whigs and Tories inflicted on one another in the South Carolina backcountry is still staggering. Many of the acts committed bordered on the barbaric, and the conduct of those who perpetrated them verged on the sadistic.

The murder of unarmed men was all too common an occurrence. The Tory John Harrison's two brothers, ill from smallpox, were shot in their beds by partisan raiders. Francis Marion's nephew, Gabriel, was captured by Tories. A shotgun was placed to his chest, and the young man was blown apart. Colonel William Washington attacked a party of Tories at Hammond's Store in Little River District. They fled without firing a shot. The Whigs pursued them and hacked a great many to death. Of the nearly 200 Tories at Hammond's Store, 150 were killed or wounded and 40 survived to become prisoners of war. At Hayes's Station, also in

Little River, Bloody Bill Cunningham set fire to a wooden structure and executed fourteen defenders as they tried to surrender.
Several were hanged, but the rest—all unarmed—were chopped
to pieces.[24]

After a 1781 engagement at Gowen's Old Fort in Spartan District, Tory militia forced the surrender of the partisan garrison.
Although they had been promised quarter if they surrendered,
many of the prisoners were tortured and killed. Those who were
not were marched into the hills to be abused or killed later. One
young member of the garrison was chained to a stake and shot. He
beseeched the Tory commander, his neighbor William "Bloody
Bill" Bates, to show mercy. "Damn you, I have nothing to do with
you" was the reply. The wounded Whig was left for dead but survived and made his escape.[25]

One of the more gruesome stories to come out of the Revolution appears in Simms's *The Partisan*. Although the work is fiction,
it is based on documentary evidence. In the tale, a Tory band
severely beats the pregnant wife of a partisan named Frampton.
The woman dies, and her death is treated rather cavalierly. When
a British officer (named Huck in the story) is asked whether he
knows that Mrs. Frampton is dead, he replies: "No—and don't
care very greatly. It's a bad breed, and the misfortune is, there's
quite too many of them. But we'll thin them soon, and easily, by
God! and the land shall be rid of the reptiles." The distraught
husband, overcome with grief, becomes a lone-wolf, a Rambo-like
figure exacting revenge on any Tory unfortunate enough to fall
into his hands.[26]

As a thirteen-year-old, Andrew Jackson witnessed similar horrors. A neighbor, driven to madness by some personal tragedy, ran
amok and hacked to death twenty Tory neighbors before he came
to his senses. Jackson's nineteenth-century biographer described
the situation in the Waxhaws: "Men hunted each other like beasts

of prey, and the savages were outdone in cruelties to the living and indignities to the dead."[27]

Not only did Jackson witness the brutal nature of the civil war in the backcountry, but he was the victim of a British officer's contempt for the Scots-Irish settlers of the Waxhaws. After the battle at Camden, Jackson fled to North Carolina with his mother and brother, Robert, to stay with relatives. Early in 1781, the Jacksons returned to their home in the Waxhaws, and Andrew and Robert rejoined a local partisan band. Attacked by the British near the Waxhaws Church, the partisans were defeated. A number were captured, but the Jackson brothers escaped into the woods. The next day they set out for their cousin's house, but a Tory neighbor betrayed them to the British.[28]

A party of dragoons surrounded the house and captured the boys. While his men were trashing the residence, the raiders' commander ordered Andrew to shine his boots. The young man refused and said, "Sir, I am a prisoner of war, and claim to be treated as such." In response, the irate officer drew his sword and tried to split open Andrew's skull. The young partisan dodged to one side but still received a nasty cut on his head and hand. The officer then ordered Robert to perform the task. He, too, refused. This time the man's aim was sure, and Robert suffered a blow to the head that very likely led to his death several months later.[29]

Grief and rage can be powerful motivating forces. So can frustration and contempt. All of these passions seemed to surface in the persons of Banastre Tarleton and James Wemyss. In late 1780, Tarleton, unable to run Francis Marion to ground, had to abandon his pursuit of the elusive Swamp Fox. Before he left the area, he burned thirty plantations to teach the locals the "Errors of Insurrection." He visited the plantation of the late General Richard Richardson and exhumed the general's corpse. Neither this effrontery nor a flogging could force Mary Cantey Richardson to reveal Marion's whereabouts. As she and her three children watched helplessly, the legionnaires took what they wanted from the Richardsons' home and barns. What they did not want, including provisions and farm animals, was locked in the barns. Then all of the buildings on the plantation were set on fire.[30]

The torch was Major James Wemyss's preferred weapon of war. Operating in the northeast section of the state from Cheraw to Georgetown, he believed that instilling fear in the residents was the best way to ensure their support of the king's cause. Cornwallis had ordered him to raise a Tory militia and to punish anyone who supported the partisans. If a partisan was captured and discovered to have broken his parole, he was to be hanged without a trial. Wemyss, like Tarleton, had little success in chasing Marion. However, he did lay waste to the countryside. He burned "scores of houses belonging to the inhabitants living on Peedee, Lynch's creek, and Black river." When Mrs. John Frierson refused to reveal where her husband was hiding, she and her four-year-old son were locked in her house, and it was set ablaze. Eventually they escaped when the heat from the fire drove the guards from the door. In an act of "mere wantonness," pigs, chickens, "and every living thing that could be caught, were thrown into the flames and burned to death."[31]

Wemyss considered Presbyterians a lesser breed in need of discipline. He labeled their houses of worship "sedition shops" and personally saw to the destruction of the Indiantown Church. When homes were ransacked, any Bibles containing the Scottish version of the Psalms were consigned to a bonfire. Despair and rage kindled a desire for revenge among those whose homes had been destroyed by the "brutal policy" of the British. As the number of burned buildings increased, so did the resolve of local partisans.[32]

The British policy was deliberate. "If warfare allows me I shall give these disturbers of the peace no quarter," Tarleton wrote Cornwallis. "If humanity obliges me to spare their lives: I shall carry them close prisoners to Camden." Three months later, he concluded: "Nothing will serve these people but fire and sword." In fact, he recommended to Cornwallis that the best way to pacify South Carolina was to follow the advice of "ancient Scripture" (and the example of Rome at Carthage) by destroying everything and salting the land.[33]

Although Tarleton was a regular army officer, his command— like those of Wemyss and Ferguson—consisted primarily of provincial regulars recruited in the northern states. On almost all occasions, local Tory militia were attached to these officers' commands and participated in the raids on their rebel neighbors. But whether the atrocities were perpetrated by regular British troops, provincial regulars, or Tory militia, they invited an Old Testament retribution from the partisans.

Brigadier General Charles O'Hara, Cornwallis's second in command, found the "violence and passions of these people are beyond every curb of religion and Humanity, they are unbounded & every hour exhibits dreadful wanton mischiefs, murders, & violences of every kind unheard of before." He reported that most of the countryside was abandoned and that those few residents who remained were "in hourly expectation of being murdered, or stripped of all their property." Although O'Hara was writing primarily about the suffering of South Carolina loyalists, the same description could have been used to describe patriot communities. The Tories had copied the tactics of their patrons, and the Whigs had responded in kind.[34]

In his Revolutionary War novels, William Gilmore Simms echoed the words of General O'Hara except that he described the Tories as having "studiously set themselves free from all restraints of humanity. . . . To burn in wantonness and to murder in cold blood, and by the cruelest tortures, were the familiar achievements of the time."[35]

The British army of occupation and its Tory allies, by unleashing the horrors of civil war on South Carolina, sowed the seeds for the defeat of their cause. Two historians of partisan warfare have noted that "[b]rutality, fear, and the resultant social disorganization can work only for the guerrillas, no matter who initiates them." This description of the impact of irregular warfare in the twentieth century could just as easily have been written about the civil war in eighteenth-century South Carolina.[36]

In December 1780, Cornwallis found it next to impossible to obtain intelligence because the partisans had "so terrified my people, that I can get nobody to venture far enough out to ascertain anything." The continual fighting had "laid waste the country," making it difficult to feed the competing forces and the local population.[37]

Backcountry Whigs and Tories, fighting for their homes and families, were responsible for some of the devastation of the countryside. However, it was the British who set the tone of the conflict. The policies that Cornwallis instituted in August and September 1780 ensured that the army of occupation and its Tory allies would have little respect for either life or property and that commanders would "take the most *vigorous* measures to *extinguish the rebellion*." And they did as ordered. If Cornwallis and his subordinates had been conducting their operations in the waning years of the twentieth century instead of during the eighteenth, they very likely would have been hauled before the International Court at the Hague as war criminals.

A century before William Tecumseh Sherman cut a swath through Georgia and South Carolina, the British practiced the same scorched-earth policy. Not only were individual residences and outbuildings burned as a matter of course, but so were towns. Goodly portions of Ninety Six, Georgetown, and Camden were destroyed before being abandoned by British garrisons. The sheer wantonness of the destruction was apparent for years after the war.

What was not burned or destroyed was stolen. There is no estimate on the value of the property confiscated by the army of occupation. Some contemporary estimates place the losses in the millions of pounds sterling. Nearly 25 percent of the state's slave labor force (much of it located in the lowcountry) disappeared. Given the average price of a slave in eighteenth-century South Carolina, a conservative estimate of their worth would be $67.5 million in today's dollars. But there is no way to estimate the value of lost livestock, furniture, houses, and barns.[38]

Nor is it possible to ever know how many men lost their lives in the dozens of unrecorded skirmishes and raids that took place in the backcountry. Although we will never know the exact number of casualties, those we do know are staggering. Of the 1,000 Americans killed in action in 1780, 66 percent died in South Carolina; of the 2,000 wounded in action, 90 percent fell in that state. In the last two years of fighting in the American Revolution, 1,089 men died in South Carolina—or 18 percent of the total American deaths for the entire war. The 2,478 wounded accounted for 31 percent of all Americans wounded during the Revolution. None of these figures include Tory casualties (many of whom were South Carolinians). "In District No. 96 alone," noted a postwar traveler, "there are twelve hundred widows."[39]

The fratricidal warfare that turned the South Carolina backcountry into what one modern historian has termed a "vast charnel house of butchered Tories and patriots" did not end in 1780. It continued for another two years until the British occupation of the state ended on 14 December 1782. But in the seven months between the fall of Charleston and the Battle of King's Mountain, the pattern of warfare—resembling a blood feud—was set. The heavy-handed tactics of the army of occupation and its Tory allies aroused the men and women of the backcountry. Their determined resistance after July 1780 derailed Clinton's grand southern strategy and helped the United States win its independence.[40]

7

Huck's Defeat
and American Independence

---

*South Carolina moved onward to independence through the
bitterest afflictions of civil war. . . . Left mainly to her own
resources, it was through bloodshed and devastation and the
depths of wretchedness that her citizens were to bring her back to
her place in the republic by their own heroic courage and self-
devotion, having suffered more, and dared more, and achieved
more than the men of any other state.*

GEORGE BANCROFT,
HISTORY OF THE UNITED STATES

I n May 1780, it appeared that Sir Henry Clinton's grand southern strategy was going to succeed. Charleston, the capital of
the "opulent, populous, and very important colony" of South
Carolina, fell. Within weeks the remainder of the forts in the
state—and their garrisons—also surrendered. Many of the leading
men in the backcountry, such as Andrew Pickens and Andrew
Williamson, took the British offer of parole. The British appeared
on the verge of being able to implement their plan to roll up the
southern states one by one and crush the rebellion.

By the end of the year, the southern strategy had come unraveled and South Carolina was anything but secure. While the British and their Tory allies occupied Charleston and various strongholds in the interior, the countryside belonged to the partisans. How did a superior force of one of the world's greatest powers lose the upper hand to a ragtag conglomeration of guerrilla fighters?

As we have seen, the British committed any number of errors in their occupation of South Carolina. Among them were the decisions not to reinstitute civil government and the revocation of paroles. A great many Carolinians, including Thomas Sumter and Richard Richardson, had given up the American cause as lost. Then Clinton issued his infamous 3 June 1780 proclamation and inadvertently brought back to life the virtually moribund revolutionary movement. This error was followed closely by a series of outrages perpetrated by the army of occupation. Tarleton's massacre at the Waxhaws was just the most widely known of any number of incidents of cruelty that inflamed the districts along the North Carolina border. The British had neither the temperament nor the leadership necessary to win the hearts and minds of the people of South Carolina.

From July 1780 until the end of the year, the Catawba River Valley and the adjacent northern districts were the scenes of some of the most brutal warfare ever fought in what is now the United States. It was a civil war, with all its horrors, as neighbors and families turned on one another with a vengeance.[1]

All who lived in the area were caught up in the maelstrom of war. The conflict did not exempt anyone on the basis of age or gender. Mary McClure and Jane Black Thomas provided crucial military information. Martha Robertson Bratton and Elizabeth Hutchinson Jackson were as willing as any man to do what they could to further the American cause. Both confronted the British to defend their families, and Elizabeth Jackson gave her life nursing neighbors imprisoned in Charleston. Andrew Jackson was just thirteen when he rode into battle with William Richardson Davie at Hanging Rock. Six months later, he was wounded and incarcerated in a British prison in Camden. It is doubtful whether there was a man, woman, or child in the northern districts who was not affected in some way by the fratricidal war that laid waste to the countryside.

Even those normally on the margins of society, such as the handicapped Joseph Kerr and the enslaved African American Watt, found themselves involved in the war against the British army of occupation. Although born crippled, Kerr was determined to do what he could to help the Whig cause. On several occasions (including the Battles of Huck's Defeat and King's Mountain), he rode into Tory camps and gathered invaluable intelligence that helped partisan leaders plan their successful attacks. Watt passed through enemy patrols to alert William Bratton of Captain Huck's whereabouts.

Such actions, while not widely known today, were indicative of the total involvement of the backcountry population in the war for American independence. Indeed, it could be argued that Jane Black Thomas's ride to warn the partisans at Cedar Springs was just as important as Paul Revere's (even though Longfellow did not immortalize her in verse as he did his forebear). Her ride of more than fifty miles through a hostile Tory countryside was truly heroic. She was willing to risk her own life to alert her family and friends to the planned British attack. As a result of her courage and pluck, the partisans were prepared and won another victory.

The men and women of the South Carolina backcountry were determined to defeat the British army of occupation and its Tory allies. They were willing to use any means necessary to achieve their goal. They dared to resist when many of their fellow citizens had given up hope and America's chief ally was considering concluding the war and giving up South Carolina to the British Empire.

Neither appeasement nor force could persuade them to submit. As a result, the backcountry was devastated by the contending forces. Farms and plantations were pillaged and burned. Little regard was shown for either property or human life. Terror bred terror; atrocity engendered atrocity; murder begat murder. South Carolina suffered "through the bitterest afflictions of civil war." But because of the grim determination of men such as William Hill, Edward Lacey, and Thomas Sumter, of women such as Martha Robertson Bratton, Jane Black Thomas, and Elizabeth Hutchinson Jackson, and of children such as Mary McClure and Andrew Jackson, Clinton's grand southern strategy faltered.

When Tarleton burned his plantation, Sumter vowed revenge. In the months after the fall of Charleston, he became an important symbol of resistance. Initially only a few men made their way to his camp across the border. In the New Acquisition, William Hill and Edward Lacey had no intention of surrendering. They rallied a few men, but even more critical was the influence of local Presbyterian clergy, such as John Simpson and William Martin, who urged their congregations to fight. The slaughter at the Waxhaws and the burning of Hill's ironworks gave the Scots-Irish of the Catawba River Valley bitter evidence of the "tender mercies of Great Britain." A number of them had long memories of British injustices in Ulster. To protect their homes and families, they joined the resistance and threw in their lot with the Gamecock.

Forming a partisan band was one thing. Inflicting damage on the British army of occupation was quite another. On 12 July 1780, at Williamson's plantation in New Acquisition District, the partisans defeated Captain Christian Huck and a detachment of the feared British Legion. It was a small battle that has sometimes been left out of the accounts of the Revolution. However, this engagement, in which more than ninety provincial regulars and Tory militia were either killed or captured, was a major turning point in the American Revolution in South Carolina.

"This victory," wrote Joseph Johnson, "was the first check given to British *troops* after the fall of Charleston; the first time that their *regulars* had been opposed by undisciplined militia." Later writers, citing letters and diaries on both sides, concurred. Just thirty days after Cornwallis had taken command of the British army in South Carolina, he suffered his first defeat. In his correspondence, the British commander seemed to have a gut feeling that Huck's Defeat was not an insignificant skirmish: "The unlucky affair that happened to the detachment of Captain Christian Huck of the Legion has given me great uneasiness."[2]

Within days Sumter had more than six hundred troops, and other partisan leaders raised the standard of resistance. Huck's Defeat was the first of thirty-five battles in which the state's freedom fighters challenged the army of occupation and its Tory allies. Of these, twenty-seven took place in the backcountry districts. From mid-July through December 1780, with the exception of the fiasco at Fishing Creek, a defeat at Long Canes, and stalemates at Rocky Mount and the Old Iron Works (Second Cedar Springs), the remaining encounters were all partisan victories. (The Battle of Camden, also an American defeat, was fought primarily by regular troops, not partisans.)[3]

During this five-and-a-half-month period, the partisans lost 497 killed or wounded and 320 prisoners of war. The British and Tory casualties were 1,200 killed or wounded and 1,286 prisoners of war. In addition, the British lost 336 men at Camden. The army of occupation could ill afford to suffer losses that were three times that of its enemy. The partisans, on the other hand, steadily increased in numbers. Each Whig victory brought in new recruits to the various partisan bands.[4]

In July, August, and September 1780, the battles in the backcountry were a reaction to the British occupation of South Carolina. Whatever the motive—idealism, revenge, or self-preservation—the result was a growing number of men and women who were willing to do whatever it took to drive the British from their communities.

Each of these engagements played a role in leading up to the decisive battle at King's Mountain. Without the partisan victories at Huck's Defeat, Stallions, Cedar Springs, Gowen's Old Fort, Earle's Ford, Prince's Fort, Thicketty Fort, Hanging Rock, and Musgrove's Mill, there would have been no battle at King's Mountain. Had these engagements—and other nameless skirmishes—not taken place, Cornwallis would have been able to march unchallenged into North Carolina.

In his memoirs, Sir Henry Clinton described Patrick Ferguson's defeat at King's Mountain as "an event which was immediately productive of the worst consequences to the King's affairs in South Carolina, and unhappily the first link in a chain of evils that followed in regular succession until they at last ended in the loss of America." Cornwallis's biographers concurred with Clinton's assessment. In describing the cairn that marked Ferguson's final resting place, they concluded that it was more than the grave of a British officer; it was "the grave of the last British hope of subduing the United States."[5]

The fighting in South Carolina did not end in October 1780 with the victory at King's Mountain. The final months of the year were a complete disaster for the British. The partisans whipped every segment of Cornwallis's army—regulars, provincial regulars, and militia. Not only was Tarleton's feared British Legion beaten in the field, but in November Tarleton himself suffered his first defeat when Sumter's partisans outmaneuvered him at Black-stock's. The next year would prove just as unsettling. After the American victory at Cowpens in January 1781, Cornwallis marched his army into North Carolina and from there to Virginia.[6]

When Cornwallis left the state in January 1781, he took with him the bulk of what remained of his army, now down to about twenty-five hundred men. In South Carolina, a handful of regulars and Tory militia still occupied the various strongholds from Ninety Six to Georgetown. By the end of the year, the British had either lost or abandoned every one of them. In Virginia, Cornwallis surrendered at Yorktown on 19 October. The British, however, still occupied Charleston and a bit of the surrounding countryside, but that was all. During 1782 there were a dozen or so engagements, the last of which occurred 14 November at Dills Bluff. Exactly one month later, the British evacuated Charleston. With them went forty-two hundred loyalists.[7]

The British had occupied Charleston for twenty months, but their planned pacification of South Carolina was never realized. Within sixty days after the fall of Charleston, the partisans inflicted the first of several dozen defeats on the army of occupation at Williamson's plantation in New Acquisition District. The partisans' defeat of Captain Christian Huck and his detachment of the feared British Legion rekindled the spirit of rebellion in the backcountry. It was but twenty miles and eighty-five days from Huck's Defeat to King's Mountain.

Clinton was only partially correct when he wrote that King's Mountain was "the first link in the chain of evils that followed in regular succession until they ended in the loss of America." There were several dozen links "in the chain of evils" before King's Mountain, and the first one was Huck's Defeat in New Acquisition District of South Carolina.

CHRONOLOGY

1756   *17 May*. The Great War for the Empire (French and Indian War) declared.

1760   *1 February*. The Cherokee War begins.

1763   *10 February*. The Peace of Paris ends the French and Indian War.

        10 November. The Treaty of Augusta with all the southern Indian nations ends Indian warfare on the frontier.

1766   *June–October*. Outlaws terrorize the frontier settlements.

1767   *June–July*. Outlaws again on the rampage.

        August. The law-abiding citizens of the backcountry form the Regulator Movement to protect themselves.

        7 November. The Regulators petition the Commons House of Assembly for redress of grievances.

1768   *June*. The Regulators agree to the "Plan of Regulation" to discipline those who disagree with them.

1769   *25 March.* The Regulators and their opponents, the Moderators, agree to end their fighting.

With peace in the backcountry, a six-year period of prosperity begins; thousands of new settlers flock to the backcountry.

1770   *14 April.* The Commons House of Assembly and royal officials disagree over the powers of the assembly.

1771   Effective royal government ceases.

1772   *September.* A party of 467 Scots-Irish families leave Ulster under the leadership of the Reverend William Martin and immigrate to the South Carolina backcountry.

1774   *6 July.* A General Meeting of representatives from all sections of the colony elect delegates to the First Continental Congress.

1775   *11 January.* The First Provincial Congress convenes.

19 April. Battles at Lexington and Concord in Massachusetts.

14 June. A Council of Safety is elected.

August–September. The Reverend William Tennent, the Reverend Oliver Hart, William Henry Drayton, Richard Richardson, and Joseph Kershaw try to win over the backcountry to the cause of the Revolution.

19 November. A band of Tories attacks the Whig garrison at Ninety Six. The first blood of the Revolution in South Carolina is shed.

December. The Snow Campaign, in which Colonel Richard Richardson and a large Whig militia army subdue the Tories, is waged.

William Hill builds his ironworks in New Acquisition District.

1776   *26 March.* South Carolina becomes the second of the original thirteen states to adopt a constitution.

28 June. The South Carolina militia repulses the British assault on Sullivan's Island.

4 July. The Declaration of Independence is signed.

July–October. The Cherokee wage an attack on the southern frontier and are defeated.

October. The beginning of a lull in the fighting that lasts for thirty months. The absence of armed conflict leads to increased settlement in the backcountry.

William and Martha Robertson Bratton build their home in New Acquisition District.

1777   *17 October.* British General John Burgoyne surrenders at Saratoga, New York.

1778   *6 February.* France signs a treaty of alliance with the United States.

28 March. The General Assembly passes a law requiring all residents to take an oath of allegiance to the state government.

April–June. A number of loyalist sympathizers flee to British Florida.

29 December. The British capture Savannah.

1779   *April.* The British enter South Carolina and reach the gates of Charleston before retreating.

1780   *January.* A British invasion fleet anchors off the South Carolina coast.

11 February. Sir Henry Clinton's army lands on John's Island.

29 March. The siege of Charleston begins.

13 April. Governor John Rutledge and three members of his council escape the besieged city.

12 May. Charleston surrenders.

May–June. Other patriot garrisons surrender across the state as militiamen take their parole and go home.

29 May. Unarmed patriot soldiers are massacred at the Waxhaws by Tarleton's British Legion.

3 June. Clinton issues a proclamation that abrogates the terms of surrender and requires all male residents to take an oath of allegiance to the king and agree to fight against their fellow countrymen.

18 June. Captain Christian Huck leads a British raiding party into New Acquisition District and burns William Hill's ironworks.

June–July. Partisan bands begin to form all along the border districts with North Carolina to resist the British occupation.

12 July. Huck's Defeat at Williamson's plantation—the first British setback in South Carolina. Engagement at Stallions—a partisan victory.

13 July. Battle at Cedar Springs—a partisan victory. Battle at Gowen's Old Fort—a partisan victory.

16 July. Action at Earle's Ford—a partisan victory. Action at Prince's Fort—a partisan victory.

20 July. Ambush at Flat Rock—a partisan victory.

30 July. Surrender at Thicketty Fort—a partisan victory.

1 August. Battle at Rocky Mount—a stalemate. Action at Hanging Rock—a partisan victory.

6 August. Battle at Hanging Rock—a partisan victory.

7 August. Second Cedar Springs—a partisan victory.

15 August. Capture of Wateree Ferry—a partisan victory.

16 August. Battle at Camden—a British victory.

18 August. Disaster at Fishing Creek—a British victory.

19 August. Battle at Musgrove's Mills—a partisan victory.

7 October. Battle at King's Mountain—a partisan victory.

9 November. Battle at Fishdam Ford—a partisan victory.

20 November. Action at Blackstock's—a partisan victory.

1781   *16 January.* Battle at Cowpens—an American victory.

19 January. Cornwallis leads his army into North Carolina to chase Nathanael Greene.

15 March. Battle of Guilford Courthouse, North Carolina.

13 May. Cornwallis crosses the Roanoke River.

19 October. Cornwallis surrenders at Yorktown.

1782   *14 December.* British forces evacuate Charleston.

1783   *23 September.* The American Revolution officially ends with the signing of the Peace of Paris.

GLOSSARY

abatis. Sharpened stakes placed around eighteenth-century fortifications to deter attacks.

Aera Furnace. The ironworks built by William Hill and Isaac Hayne in New Acquisition District.

backcountry. The area of South Carolina from about fifty miles inland to the mountains (see also *lowcountry*).

British Legion. A cavalry regiment of provincial troops from New York and Pennsylvania under the command of Lieutenant Colonel Banastre Tarleton.

Catawba River Valley. A swath of territory that runs from near Camden in South Carolina to Salisbury in North Carolina; the scene of much of the Revolutionary War fighting in the backcountry.

Commons House of Assembly. The lower house of the colonial legislature, elected by the people.

Council of Safety. An arm of the Provincial Congress charged with the defense of South Carolina.

dragoon. A cavalryman.

Fairforest. A community in Spartan District.

General Assembly. The legislature of the state of South Carolina.

General Meeting. One of many extralegal gatherings that arose in the 1770s; the General Meeting of 6 July 1774 led directly to the formation of a revolutionary party in South Carolina.

Great Wagon Road. The main avenue of immigration for thousands of new settlers; the road that began in Pennsylvania near Philadelphia, traversed the Shenandoah Valley of Virginia and the piedmont of North Carolina, and ended in the South Carolina backcountry (see also *Catawba River Valley* and *Waxhaws, the*).

High Hills of the Santee. The rolling terrain in the middle section of the state on the upper reaches of the Santee River and its tributaries.

Huck's Defeat. The name given the patriot victory at James Williamson's plantation in New Acquisition District; the first British defeat after the fall of Charleston.

Little River District. A district located between Spartan and Ninety Six Districts. (It included portions of present-day Laurens and Newberry Counties.)

lowcountry. The coastal rice and indigo plantation area of South Carolina stretching about fifty miles inland (see also *backcountry*).

loyalists. Americans who chose to fight for the king (see also *Tories*).

militia. Volunteers on both sides whose term of enlistment might range from several days (the duration of an engagement) to several months.

Moderators. A vigilante band formed in the late 1760s by those who opposed the excesses of the Regulators (see *Regulators*).

New Acquisition District. A district in the Catawba River Valley along the North Carolina border; the scene of much of the fighting in 1780; sometimes referred to as "the New Acquisition." (It included present-day York County.)

Ninety Six District. A large district along the Savannah River that contained a sizable number of loyalists; there was an important fort at the courthouse town of Ninety Six. (The district included portions of present-day Abbeville, Aiken, Edgefield, Greenwood, McCormick, and Saluda Counties.)

Over Mountain Men. Residents of what is now Tennessee who crossed over the mountains to fight the British, most notably at the Battle of King's Mountain.

parole. Captured soldiers were released to return home upon agreeing not to fight anymore.

partisans. Militia units that fought a guerrilla or partisan war against the British army of occupation.

patriots. Americans who fought for the cause of independence (see also *Whigs*).

Prince of Wales Regiment. A provincial regiment.

Provincial Congress. South Carolina's revolutionary legislature (1775–76).

provincial troops. Americans who enlisted in British army units to fight during the Revolution; sometimes referred to as "provincial regulars" to distinguish them from Tory militia and from British units (see *British Legion*).

quarter. Accepting a defeated foe's surrender with the assurance not to harm him (see *Tarleton's quarter*).

rangers. Mounted colonial militia with wide-ranging police powers to subdue outlaws.

rebels. The term the British and Tories applied to all who opposed the army of occupation in South Carolina.

regulars. Military units from Great Britain.

Regulators. A vigilante group formed in the mid-1760s by the backcountry's leading citizens to protect themselves from the outlaw bands (see *Moderators*).

Snow Campaign. The December 1775 backcountry expedition that successfully subdued a Tory uprising.

South Carolina Royalists. A provincial regiment made up primarily of South Carolina Tories.

Spartan District. A border district in the northwestern portion of the state. (It included portions of present-day Spartanburg and Union Counties.)

Tarleton's quarter. The murder of unarmed prisoners after they surrendered; the term came into common usage after Banastre Tarleton's troops massacred POWs at the Waxhaws.

Tories. Americans who chose to fight for the king (see also *loyalists*).

Ulster. The counties of northern Ireland whence came many of the Scots-Irish immigrants who settled in the South Carolina backcountry.

Waxhaws, the. A section of the borderlands between North and South Carolina settled primarily by Scots-Irish; the site of Tarleton's massacre of unarmed POWs.

Whigs. Americans who fought for the cause of independence (see also *patriots*).

BIOGRAPHICAL INFORMATION

Adamson, John. A Tory militia captain from Camden whose intervention saved the life of Martha Robertson Bratton; in turn, after Huck's Defeat, she saved his.

Arbuthnot, Marriott. A British admiral and commander of the fleet that besieged Charleston in 1780.

Bratton, Martha Robertson. A native of North Carolina who with her husband moved to New Acquisition District in the 1770s; she was one of the backcountry heroines of the Revolution who came to symbolize both defiance (of Captain Huck) and mercy (saving a Tory officer's life and nursing him back to health).

Bratton, William. A native of Virginia who moved to New Acquisition District in the 1770s; he became a leading member of the community and a colonel in the militia; after the fall of Charleston, he and his neighbors formed one of the first partisan resistance groups in the backcountry; he participated in the Battle of Huck's Defeat.

Brown, Thomas. A Georgia Tory whose opposition to the Revolution led to his being tortured, tarred, and feathered; thereafter he was known as "Burnfoot" Brown and became a colonel in the Tory militia; he showed little mercy to any Whigs unfortunate enough to fall into his grasp.

Campbell, William. One of the Over Mountain Men from what is now Tennessee who was chosen by his fellow militia leaders to be the commander of the partisan forces at King's Mountain.

Clinton, Sir Henry. A British general and commander of British forces in the American theater of operations; he personally commanded the abortive expedition against Charleston in 1776 and the successful one in 1780 that led to the capture of the city; his 3 June 1780 proclamation abrogating the terms of surrender was the spark that ignited the resistance movement in the state.

Cornwallis, Charles, Lord. A British general and commander of the British army of occupation in South Carolina; although he initially declared that the army should treat civilians with respect, he did little to curb the atrocities of his subordinates; by the end of the summer of 1780, he had ordered draconian measures in a vain attempt to suppress the resistance; those measures failed, and he took a seriously weakened army into North Carolina and thence to Yorktown and defeat.

Cunningham, William. A loyalist militia officer known as "Bloody Bill" for his cold-blooded treatment of captured Whigs; a resident of the District Between the Broad and Saluda Rivers.

DeKalb, Jean. A native of Bavaria who served in the French army and then came to the United States to fight in the Revolution; the Continental Congress commissioned him a major general; he was killed at the Battle of Camden.

Ferguson, Patrick. A Scottish major and commander of Tory militia units in the backcountry; his threats against the Over Mountain Men led to their crossing into South Carolina and joining with local militia to defeat his force at the Battle of King's Mountain, where he was killed.

Fletchell, Thomas. One of the leading citizens of the Fairforest community and a militia colonel; he and a number of other members of the Fairforest Baptist Church followed their minister into supporting the king's cause.

Gates, Horatio. An American general and hero of the Battle of Saratoga; following the surrender of Charleston, he was given command of the southern army and foolishly forced a confrontation with Cornwallis at Camden; in the midst of the battle, he jumped on his horse and hightailed it to North Carolina.

Greene, Nathanael. Commander of the Continental forces in South Carolina, succeeding Gates; his understanding of the concept of mobile warfare and his wise use of the partisans led to the eventual liberation of South Carolina.

Hill, William. A native of Belfast, he settled in New Acquisition District, where his Aera Furnace produced farm implements for the nearby residents; with the outbreak of war, he converted the furnace to producing arms, and Hill's Iron works was one of the primary targets of Captain Huck's raid; as a colonel in the militia, he helped organize one of the first partisan bands in the backcountry; he participated in a number of battles, including Rocky Mount, Hanging Rock, King's Mountain, and Cowpens.

Huck, Christian. A Quaker attorney from Philadelphia who became a loyalist; as a captain in the feared British Legion, he led two raids into New Acquisition District; during the first one, he antagonized the local populace; during the second, he was killed in a battle at Williamson's plantation that was known thereafter as Huck's Defeat—the first setback for the British army of occupation.

Jackson, Andrew. The future president was a native of the Waxhaws and a teenage partisan with William Richardson Davie at Hanging Rock; he was wounded, captured, and imprisoned by the British.

Jackson, Elizabeth Hutchinson. A native of County Antrim, Ulster, Andrew Jackson's mother moved with her husband to South Carolina to be near her family in the Waxhaws; she nursed the wounded after the battle at the Waxhaws and died after going to Charleston to nurse neighbors imprisoned aboard ships in the harbor.

Kerr, Joseph. A crippled resident of the Catawba River Valley who, despite his handicap, joined a local partisan band and served as a spy; prior to Huck's Defeat and King's Mountain, he provided the partisans with crucial military intelligence.

Kershaw, Joseph. A native of Yorkshire who was in South Carolina by the mid-1750s; he became a successful merchant, entrepreneur, and planter in Camden; one of the leading revolutionaries in the backcountry, he suffered tremendous property losses during the British occupation.

Lacey, Edward. A native of Pennsylvania who moved to the Catawba River Valley before the Revolution; although he was an ardent patriot, his father and brother were Tories; he was a partisan captain; he commanded one of the units at Huck's Defeat and participated in a dozen other battles, including King's Mountain.

Lincoln, Benjamin. An American general and commander of the Continental army in South Carolina; his ill-conceived plan of defense resulted in the fall of Charleston and the surrender of his army—the worst defeat the Americans suffered during the war; he was exchanged and was with George Washington at Yorktown and actually received the sword of surrender.

Marion, Francis. A native South Carolinian and resident of the lowcountry; after the fall of Charleston, he became a major figure in the resistance movement and led his partisans against the British in the swamps of the coastal plain; because of his elusiveness, he was known as "the Swamp Fox."

Martin, William. A native of Ulster and Presbyterian clergyman who led a large number of Ulster families to South Carolina in 1772; he was pastor of the Rocky Creek Church; a passionate Whig, he was imprisoned in Camden for his pro-revolutionary sermons.

McClure, Mary. A teenager who slipped away from Captain Huck's raiding party and warned her father of the British activities.

McDowell, Charles. A North Carolina militia general and commander of one of the partisan bands operating in the backcountry; he was a link with Shelby and the Over Mountain Men.

Moultrie, William. A revolutionary military leader and commander of the fort on Sullivan's Island, 28 June 1776; after the American victory, the fort was renamed in his honor; he rose to the rank of general and was the first president of the Society of the Cincinnati in South Carolina.

Mulkey, Philip. A Baptist clergyman and founder of the Fairforest Baptist Church in Spartan District—one of the denomination's mother churches in the backcountry; with the outbreak of the Revolution, he sided with the king's cause and convinced a number of his congregation to follow suit.

Prevost, Augustine. A British general and commander of the expedition into South Carolina in 1779.

Richardson, Richard. A native of Virginia who immigrated to South Carolina in the 1730s; he settled in the High Hills, where he became a leading planter; in 1768 he helped end the conflict between the Regulators and the

Moderators; in 1775 the Council of Safety ordered him to suppress the Tory uprising, which he did in the famous Snow Campaign; as a former brigadier general, he was imprisoned by the British in 1780, and he died as a result of his incarceration.

Rutledge, John. A wealthy Charleston lawyer and political figure, he was governor of South Carolina 1776–78 and 1779–82; during the British occupation, the General Assembly gave him unlimited authority to rule the state, and he was, in effect, the revolutionary government of South Carolina; a signer of the Constitution of the United States.

Shelby, Isaac. A North Carolina militia colonel and one of the key figures at the Battle of King's Mountain.

Simpson, John. A Presbyterian clergyman and ardent revolutionary; after preaching a sermon to his Fishing Creek congregation urging them to fight the British, he took up his musket and joined Sumter's partisans; he was one of the targets of Captain Huck's raiding party.

Stedman, Charles. A Tory officer who served as commissary general for the British army of occupation.

Sumter, Thomas. A native of Virginia who moved to South Carolina in the 1760s; after the fall of Charleston, he retired to his plantation in the High Hills, but after the British destroyed his home, he took up arms as a partisan; he participated in numerous battles, including Fishing Creek, Fishdam Ford, and Blackstock's; he held the rank of brigadier general and was known by his men as "the Gamecock"; although his military record was spotty, he was an important rallying point and symbol of the resistance against the army of occupation.

Tarleton, Banastre. A British officer (major; lieutenant colonel) and commander of the feared British Legion; his cruel and contemptuous treatment of the local populace gave rise to the partisan resistance in the border districts.

Thomas, Jane Black. A resident of Spartan District and the wife of John Thomas, the commander of the Spartan Regiment; while nursing him in prison at Ninety Six, she overheard plans for a Tory military operation and rode all night to warn her family and friends.

Turnbull, George. A Tory lieutenant colonel of the New York Volunteers and commander of the British stronghold at Rocky Mount.

Watt. An enslaved African American owned by the Brattons; during Huck's second raid, he dodged enemy patrols to get word of the location of the Tory camp to William Bratton.

Wemyss, James. A British officer whose announced policy of burning Presbyterian churches as "sedition shops" fueled the resistance movement in the backcountry.

Williams, James. A native of New Hanover County, Virginia; he moved to South Carolina in 1773 and settled in Little River District; he rose to the rank of general in militia; he was killed at the Battle of King's Mountain.

Williamson, Andrew. A backcountry militia general whose surrender after the fall of Charleston did much to convince the British that South Carolina was a conquered province.

Winn, Richard. A native of Fauquier County, Virginia, who settled in South Carolina in 1768; he participated in the battle at Sullivan's Island and after the British capture of Charleston joined Thomas Sumter's partisan band.

Woodmason, Charles. An Anglican missionary in the backcountry in the 1750s and 1760s; his journal is one of the most famous accounts of life on the southern frontier; during the Regulator Movement, he helped draft the petition to the Commons House of Assembly.

NOTES

INTRODUCTION

1. Alice Hanson Jones, *Wealth of a Nation to Be: The American Colonies on the Eve of the Revolution* (New York: Columbia University Press, 1980), 10, 170–71, 377–79.
2. United Nations, "Statute of the International Tribunal," adopted 25 May 1993; as amended 13 May 1998. Available at: www.un.org/icty/basic/statut/statute.htm.
3. John Buchanan, *The Road to Guilford Courthouse: The American Revolution in the Carolinas* (New York: John Wiley & Sons, 1997), 105–6. Don Higginbotham, *War of American Independence: Military Attitudes, Policies, and Practice, 1763–1789*, a Classics Edition (1971; Boston: Northeastern University Press, 1983), 360–62. Jerome J. Nadelhaft, *The Disorders of War: The Revolution in South Carolina* (Orono: University of Maine at Orono Press, 1981), 58–68. Franklin Wickwire and Mary Wickwire, *Cornwallis: The American Adventure* (Boston: Houghton Mifflin, 1970), 170. Robert M. Calhoon, *The Loyalists in Revolutionary America, 1760–1781* (New York: Harcourt Brace Jovanovich, 1973), 492–93. Hugh C. Holman, "William Gilmore Simms' Picture of the Revolution as a Civil Conflict," *Journal of Southern History* 15 (November 1949): 449. William Gilmore Simms, *Eutaw*, published for the Southern Studies Program, University of South Carolina (reprint,

Spartanburg: Reprint Co., 1976), 68. *South-Carolina in the Revolutionary War* by a Southron [William Gilmore Simms] (Charleston: Walker & James, 1853), 14. William Gilmore Simms, *Joscelyn*, published for the Southern Studies Program, University of South Carolina (1867; reprint, Spartanburg, S.C.: Reprint Cor, 1976), 5.

4. George Bancroft, *History of the United States*, 11th ed., 10 vols. (Boston: Little, Brown and Co., 1875), 10:300.

5. Cornwallis quoted in Wickwire and Wickwire, *Cornwallis*, 174–75. Peter Paret and John W. Shy, *Guerrillas in the 1960s*, quoted in Russell F. Weigley, *The Partisan War: The South Carolina Campaign of 1780–1782*, Tricentennial booklet 2, published for the South Carolina Tricentennial Commission (Columbia: University of South Carolina Press, 1970), 10.

ONE

1. Walter Edgar, *South Carolina: A History* (Columbia: University of South Carolina Press, 1998), 342–43.

2. John M. Barry, *Natural Vegetation of South Carolina* (Columbia: University of South Carolina Press, 1980), 55–94. George Howe, *History of the Presbyterian Church in South Carolina*, 2 vols. (Columbia: Duffie & Chapman, 1879, 1883), 1:296.

3. Barry, *Natural Vegetation of South Carolina*, 72. Charles M. Kovacik and John J. Winberry, *South Carolina: A Geography* (Boulder, CO: Westview Press, 1987), 43. Howe, *History of the Presbyterian Church*, 1:296.

4. Works Projects Administration, *South Carolina: The WPA Guide to the Palmetto State*, with a new introduction by Walter B. Edgar (1941; reprint, Columbia: University of South Carolina Press, 1988), 16–17. Alexander Sprunt Jr. and E. Burnham Chamberlain, *South Carolina Bird Life*, rev. ed. (Columbia: University of South Carolina Press, 1970), 1, 289–90. Bobby Gilmer Moss, *The Old Iron District: A Study of the Development of Cherokee County, 1750–1897* (Clinton, SC: Jacobs Press, 1972), 2. Edgar, *South Carolina*, 12–13.

5. Kovacik and Winberry, *South Carolina: A Geography*, 40. Barry, *Natural Vegetation of South Carolina*, 55–94. Carl Bridenbaugh, *Myths and Realities: Societies of the Colonial South* (1952; reprint, New York: Atheneum, 1968), 121.

6. Bridenbaugh, *Myths and Realities*, 129. Louise Pettus, assisted by Nancy Crockett, *The Waxhaws* (Rock Hill, SC: Regal Graphics, 1993), 6–7, 12.

7. Bridenbaugh, *Myths and Realities*, 127–29; quote, 127–28. Pettus, *The Waxhaws*, 2.

8. Bridenbaugh, *Myths and Realities*, 121–31. Richard Maxwell Brown, *The South Carolina Regulators* (Cambridge, MA: Belknap Press of Harvard University Press, 1963), 2–3. Rachel N. Klein, *Unification of a Slave State: The*

Rise of the Planter Class in the South Carolina Backcountry, 1760–1808, published for the Institute of Early American History and Culture, Williamsburg, VA (Chapel Hill: University of North Carolina Press, 1990), 14. Irving H. Bartlett, *John C. Calhoun: A Biography* (New York: W. W. Norton & Co., 1993), 20–22. Howe, *History of the Presbyterian Church*, 1:296–97. Pettus, *The Waxhaws*, 7–8.

9. Maldwyn A. Jones, "The Scotch Irish in British America," in Bernard Bailyn and Philip D. Morgan, eds., *Strangers Within the Realm: Cultural Margins of the First British Empire*, published for the Institute of Early American History and Culture, Williamsburg, VA (Chapel Hill: University of North Carolina Press, 1991), 291–93. Edgar, *South Carolina*, 88–91. Anne Pickens Collins, *A Goodly Heritage: History of Chester County, South Carolina* (Columbia, SC: Collins Publishers, 1986), 11–12, 20–21.

10. Bridenbaugh, *Myths and Realities*, 133.

11. Collins, *A Goodly Heritage*, 9–12, 20–21.

12. Ibid., 20–21. Maurice S. Ulmer, *The Covenanters of Fairfield County: A History of the Richmond Reformed Presbyterian Church* (Lancaster, SC: Craftsman Press, 1996), 5. Maurice S. Ulmer, *The Covenanters of Chester County, South Carolina: A History of the Rocky Creek Reformed Presbyterian Church* (Lancaster, SC: Craftsman Press, 1997), 9.

13. Edward McCrady, *The History of South Carolina Under the Royal Government, 1719–1776* (New York: Macmillan, 1901), 317n, 318n. Edgar, *South Carolina*, 90. Moss, *The Old Iron District*, 5–6. Sam Thomas, "The 1780 Presbyterian Rebellion and the Battle of Huck's Defeat" (unpublished manuscript 1996, York County Historical Commission, York, SC), passim. Jones, "The Scotch Irish in British America," 293.

14. Bartlett, *John C. Calhoun*, 20–21. Klein, *Unification of a Slave State*, 14–15. McCrady, *South Carolina Under Royal Government*, 315–16. Robert V. Remini, *Andrew Jackson and the Course of American Empire, 1767–1821* (New York: Harper & Row, 1977), 1–5. Robert V. Remini, *The Life of Andrew Jackson* (1988; New York: Penguin Books, 1990), 4–5. Marquis James, *The Life of Andrew Jackson* (Indianapolis: Bobbs-Merrill Co., 1938), 3–8.

15. Moss, *The Old Iron District*, 7.

16. Ibid., 44–45. Ben Robertson, *Red Hills and Cotton* (1942; reprint, Columbia: University of South Carolina Press, 1991), 193–97.

17. Bridenbaugh, *Myths and Realities*, 140–41. Moss, *The Old Iron District*, 7–8. Suzanne Cameron Linder, "A River in Time: A Cultural Study of the Yadkin/Pee Dee River System to 1825" (Ph.D. diss., University of South Carolina, 1993), 96–99. Jones, "The Scotch Irish in British America," 299.

18. Linder, "A River in Time," 96–98. David Ramsay, *History of South Carolina* (Charleston: David Longworth, 1808, 1809; reprint, Newberry, SC: W. J. Duffie, 1858), 2:246–50. James H. Merrell, *The Indians' New World:*

Catawbas and Their Neighbors from European Contact Through the Era of Removal, published for the Institute of Early American History and Culture, Williamsburg, VA (Chapel Hill: University of North Carolina Press, 1989), 173. Moss, *The Old Iron District*, 7–8.

19. Richard J. Hooker, ed., *The Carolina Backcountry on the Eve of the Revolution: The Journal and Other Writings of Charles Woodmason, Anglican Itinerant*, published for the Institute of Early American History and Culture, Williamsburg, VA (Chapel Hill: University of North Carolina Press, 1953), 7, 32, 33. Bridenbaugh, *Myths and Realities*, 130–31.

20. Hooker, *The Carolina Backcountry on the Eve of the Revolution*, 32, 33. Ramsay, *History of South Carolina*, 2:246–50. Merrell, *The Indians' New World*, 173. Bridenbaugh, *Myths and Realities*, 139–40, 176. Pettus, *The Waxhaws*, 14–15.

21. Hooker, *The Carolina Backcountry on the Eve of the Revolution*, 13, 34, 39, 52, 196. Moss, *The Old Iron District*, 8, 12–14. Pettus, *The Waxhaws*, 15–16.

22. Hooker, *The Carolina Backcountry on the Eve of the Revolution*, 39. Moss, *The Old Iron District*, 12.

23. Hooker, *The Carolina Backcountry on the Eve of the Revolution*, 31–33, 61. Linder, "A River in Time," 64. Brown, *The South Carolina Regulators*, 31.

24. Lacy K. Ford, *Origins of Southern Radicalism: The South Carolina Upcountry, 1800–1860* (New York: Oxford University Press, 1988), 19–20. Bridenbaugh, *Myths and Realities*, 180–85.

25. Jones, "The Scotch Irish in British America," 302–3. Hooker, *The Carolina Backcountry on the Eve of the Revolution*, 16–17, 20, 30–31, 34, 39, 44–47, 75, 108. Pettus, *The Waxhaws*, 7. Allen D. Charles, *The Narrative History of Union County, South Carolina*, published for the Union County Historical Commission and Arthur State Bank (Spartanburg, SC: Reprint Co., 1987), 8–9.

26. Hooker, *The Carolina Backcountry on the Eve of the Revolution*, 45, 58, 62, 80–81. Thomas, "The 1780 Presbyterian Rebellion," passim.

27. Ford, *Origins of Southern Radicalism*, 19–21. Brown, *The South Carolina Regulators*, 20–22. Leah Townsend, *South Carolina Baptists* (Florence, SC: Florence Printing Co., 1935), 272–73. Howe, *History of the Presbyterian Church*, 1:285–99, 363.

28. J. D. Bailey, *Reverends Philip Mulkey and James Fowler: The Story of the First Baptist Church Planted in Upper South Carolina* (Cowpens, SC: n.p., 1941), 3–6. Charles, *The Narrative History of Union County*, 11–12. Townsend, *South Carolina Baptists*, 126. Edgar, *South Carolina*, 183.

29. Hooker, *The Carolina Backcountry on the Eve of the Revolution*, 47.

30. Brown, *The South Carolina Regulators*, 13–24. Hooker, ed., *The Carolina Backcountry on the Eve of the Revolution*, 123–29.

31. Edgar, *South Carolina*, 344.

32. Jones, "The Scotch Irish in British America," 296.

33. Brown, *The South Carolina Regulators*, 4–5.

34. Ibid., 4–8; quote, 6.

35. Ibid., 4–8. Edgar, *South Carolina*, 345–48. For monetary conversion details, see ibid., 62n.

36. Edgar, *South Carolina*, 346–48.

37. Ibid., 355–57. Brown, *The South Carolina Regulators*, 27–38.

38. Edgar, *South Carolina*, 356–57.

39. Brown, *The South Carolina Regulators*, 34–35.

40. Edgar, *South Carolina*, 358.

41. Brown, *The South Carolina Regulators*, 26–27. Hooker, *The Carolina Backcountry on the Eve of Revolution*, passim. Ford, *Origins of Southern Radicalism*, 20–21.

42. Klein, *Unification of a Slave State*, 68–69. Brown, *The South Carolina Regulators*, 24–27, 113–19.

43. Hooker, *The Carolina Backcountry on the Eve of the Revolution*, 213–30.

44. Ibid., 214–15.

45. Ibid., 230–33.

46. Brown, *The South Carolina Regulators*, 43–47.

47. Hooker, *The Carolina Backcountry on the Eve of the Revolution*, 227.

48. Brown, *The South Carolina Regulators*, 47–52.

49. Ibid.

50. Ibid., 88–89.

51. Ibid., 83–95.

52. Ibid., 53–63.

53. Ibid., 83–95.

54. Klein, *Unification of a Slave State*, 8–34. Laurens quoted in Edgar, *South Carolina*, 248.

55. Klein, *Unification of a Slave State*, 24–26.

56. Ibid., 29–34. Moss, *The Old Iron District*, 9–10.

57. N. Louise Bailey and Elizabeth Ivey Cooper, *Biographical Directory of the South Carolina House of Representatives*, vol. 3, *1775–1790* (Columbia: University of South Carolina Press, 1981), 339. J. D. Bailey, *Commanders at King's Mountain* (Gaffney, SC: Ed. H. DeCamp, 1926), 202. "Early Ironworks of Northwestern South Carolina," a National Register of Historic Places Inventory-Nomination, on file in the South Carolina Department of Archives and History, Columbia.

58. Klein, *Unification of a Slave State*, 35–36. Edgar, *South Carolina*, 337. Walter B. Edgar and N. Louise Bailey, *Biographical Directory of the South Carolina House of Representatives*, vol. 2, *The Commons House of Assembly, 1692–1775* (Columbia: University of South Carolina Press, 1977), 380–82.

59. Bailey and Cooper, *Biographical Directory of the South Carolina House of Representatives*, 3:708–9. Howe, *History of the Presbyterian Church in South Carolina*, 1:533.
60. Virginia G. Meynard, *The Venturers: The Hampton, Harrison, and Earle Families of Virginia, South Carolina, and Texas* (Easley, SC: Southern Historical Press, 1981), ii, 2–67. Bailey and Cooper, *Biographical Directory of the South Carolina House of Representatives*, 3:303–11.
61. Meynard, *The Venturers*, 58–71.
62. Wade Buice Fairey, *Historic Brattonsville: A Wedge of County History* (York, SC: York County Historical Commission, 1993), 3–4.
63. Ibid., 4.
64. Later the original Fishing Creek Presbyterian Church was called Lower Fishing Creek Church. Howe, *History of the Presbyterian Church*, 1: 297. Fairey, *Historic Brattonsville*, 4–5.
65. Hooker, *The Carolina Backcountry on the Eve of the Revolution*, 247–78.

TWO

1. Edgar, *South Carolina*, 218–19.
2. Ibid., 219–23.
3. Robert A. Olwell, " 'Domestick Enemies': Slavery and Political Independence in South Carolina, May 1775–March 1776," *Journal of Southern History* 55 (1989): 33–34. Robert M. Weir, *Colonial South Carolina: A History*, in *A History of the American Colonies*, 13 vols., Milton M. Klein and Jacob E. Cooke, general editors (Millwood, NY: KTO Press, 1983), 200–203. Edward McCrady, *The History of the Revolution in South Carolina, 1775–1780* (New York: Macmillan, 1901), 182–85.
4. Thomas Fletchell to Henry Laurens, 24 July 1775, in Robert W. Gibbes, ed., *Documentary History of the American Revolution*, 3 vols. (1855; reprint, Spartanburg, SC: Reprint Co., 1972), 1:123–24. Thomas H. Pope, *The History of Newberry County, South Carolina, vol. 1, 1749–1860* (Columbia: University of South Carolina Press, 1973), 43. Robert Stansbury Lambert, *South Carolina Loyalists in the American Revolution* (Columbia: University of South Carolina Press, 1987), 35–41. J. B. O. Landrum, *Colonial and Revolutionary History of Upper South Carolina* (Greenville, SC: Shannon & Co., 1897), 50. Charles, *The Narrative History of Union County*, 27–28.

For an excellent fictional account (based upon historical documentation) of the difficulty of choosing sides, see Simms, *Joscelyn*, 7–25. Holman, "William Gilmore Simms' Picture of the Revolution as a Civil Conflict," 441–45.
5. Rachel N. Klein, "Frontier Planters and the American Revolution: The South Carolina Backcountry, 1775–1782," in Ronald Hoffman, Thad W.

Tate, and Peter J. Albert, eds., *An Uncivil War: The Southern Backcountry During the American Revolution*, published for the United States Capitol Historical Society (Charlottesville: University Press of Virginia, 1985), 40–44. Jones, "The Scotch Irish in British America," 309–10. Pope, *The History of Newberry County, South Carolina*, 43. Joseph Johnson, *Traditions and Reminiscences Chiefly of the American Revolution in the South* (1851; reprint, Spartanburg, SC: Reprint Co., 1972), 140–41. Charles, *The Narrative History of Union County*, 30–31. Collins, *A Goodly Heritage*, 32.

6. Klein, *Unification of a Slave State*, 80–85. Klein, "Frontier Planters and the American Revolution," 42.

7. Klein, "Frontier Planters and the American Revolution," 42–48. Klein, *Unification of a Slave State*, 80–85.

8. "A Fragment of a Journal Kept by Rev. William Tennent . . . ," in Gibbes, *Documentary History of the American Revolution*, 1:228. Buchanan, *The Road to Guilford Courthouse*, 95–96. Calhoon, *The Loyalists in Revolutionary America*, 448–57. Lewis P. Jones, *The South Carolina Civil War of 1775* (Lexington, SC: Sandlapper Store, 1975), 37–55.

9. "A Fragment of a Journal Kept by Rev. William Tennent . . . ," 2:225–39; quote, 227. Charles, *The Narrative History of Union County*, 27–28, 30.

10. Lambert, *South Carolina Loyalists in the American Revolution*, 38–42. Buchanan, *The Road to Guilford Courthouse*, 95–100. Jones, *The South Carolina Civil War of 1775*, 30–32. Pope, *The History of Newberry County*, 1:43–45.

11. William Henry Drayton to Council of Safety, 21 August 1776, in Gibbes, *Documentary History of the American Revolution*, 2:150. Lambert, *South Carolina Loyalists in the American Revolution*, 39–42, 219. McCrady, *The History of South Carolina in the Revolution, 1775–1780*, 64–65. Landrum, *Colonial and Revolutionary History of Upper South Carolina*, 44–45. John Drayton, *Memoirs of the American Revolution as Relates to the State of South Carolina*, in *Eyewitness Accounts of the American Revolution*, 2 vols. (1821; reprint, New York: New York Times/Arno Press, 1969), 2:28–34. Charles, *The Narrative History of Union County*, 25–26.

12. Lambert, *South Carolina Loyalists in the American Revolution*, 42–43. Anne King Gregorie, *Thomas Sumter* (Columbia, SC: R. L. Bryan Co., 1931), 40. Buchanan, *The Road to Guilford Courthouse*, 100–103.

13. Pope, *The History of Newberry County*, 1:45.

14. "Declaration by Col. Richardson to Insurgents Under Cunningham," in Gibbes, *Documentary History of the American Revolution*, 2:224–25. Archie Vernon Huff Jr., *Greenville: The History of the City and County in the South Carolina Piedmont* (Columbia: University of South Carolina Press, 1995), 20–23. David Duncan Wallace, *The History of South Carolina*, 4 vols. (New York: American Historical Society, 1934), 2:145–48. Charles, *The Narrative History of Union County*, 30–31.

15. J. H. Easterby, ed., *Basic Documents of South Carolina: The Constitution of 1776* (Columbia: Historical Commission of South Carolina, n.d.).

16. Henry Lumpkin, *From Savannah to Yorktown: The American Revolution in the South* (Columbia: University of South Carolina Press, 1981), 10–18. Wallace, *The History of South Carolina*, 2:154–59.

17. Wallace, *The History of South Carolina*, 2:134–59; Campbell quote, Higginbotham, *War of American Independence*, 136–37.

18. Robertson, *Red Hills and Cotton*, 199. Meynard, *The Venturers*, 72–73. Landrum, *Colonial and Revolutionary History of Upper South Carolina*, 86–89.

19. Lambert, *South Carolina Loyalists in the American Revolution*, 51–53.

20. Drayton quoted in Huff, *Greenville*, 25. Lambert, *South Carolina Loyalists in the American Revolution*, 51–54. Wallace, *The History of South Carolina*, 2:164–67. Huff, *Greenville*, 24–26. McCrady, *The History of South Carolina in the Revolution, 1775–1780*, 200–201. Townsend, *South Carolina Baptists*, 179.

21. Wallace, *The History of South Carolina*, 2:167. Work Projects Administration (Spartanburg Unit of the Writers' Program), *A History of Spartanburg County* (reprint, Spartanburg, SC: Spartanburg Branch of the American Association of University Women, 1940), 25–26. Pope, *The History of Newberry County*, 1:46. William Johnson, *Sketches of the Life and Correspondence of Nathanael Greene*, in *The Era of the American Revolution*, Leonard W. Levy, general editor, 2 vols. (1822; reprint, New York: DaCapo Press, 1973), 1:268–69, 279.

22. Moss, *The Old Iron District*, 22, 26, 44–45. Wallace, *The History of South Carolina*, 2:167. Work Projects Administration, *A History of Spartanburg County*, 25–26. Pope, *The History of Newberry County*, 1:46. Collins, *A Goodly Heritage*, 55.

23. Walter B. Edgar, ed., *Biographical Directory of the South Carolina House of Representatives, vol. 1, Session Lists, 1692–1973* (Columbia: University of South Carolina Press, 1974), 181, 186. Bailey and Cooper, *Biographical Directory of the South Carolina House of Representatives*, 3:32, 62, 90, 116–17, 273, 306–7, 328–29, 350–52, 461–62, 488, 505–6, 581–82, 664, 786.

24. Landrum, *Colonial and Revolutionary History of Upper South Carolina*, 170–71. James Williams to Daniel Williams, 12 June 1779; Williams to Andrew Williamson, 4 January 1780, both in Gibbes, *Documentary History of the American Revolution* (Baltimore: Genealogical Publishing Co., 1983), 3:115–18. Bobby Gilmer Moss, *Roster of South Carolina Patriots in the American Revolution*, 995.

25. Fairey, *Historic Brattonsville*, 7.

26. Ibid., 4, 7–9. Elizabeth F. Ellet, *Heroic Women of the Revolution* (Philadelphia: n.p., 1848), 244. Samuel Thomas, York County Historical Commission, conversation with the author, 13 March 1998.

27. Bailey and Cooper, *Biographical Directory of the South Carolina House of Rep-*

resentatives, 3:339. Bailey, *Commanders at King's Mountain*, 202. "Early Iron-works of Northwestern South Carolina," National Register of Historic Places Inventory—Nomination Form, 1987, South Carolina Department of Archives and History, Columbia, South Carolina.

28. Ibid.

29. George C. Rogers Jr., *Charleston in the Age of the Pinckneys* (Norman: University of Oklahoma Press, 1969), 45. Walter J. Fraser, *Charleston! Charleston!: The History of a Southern City* (Columbia: University of South Carolina Press, 1989), 155–56. McCrady, *The History of South Carolina in the Revolution, 1775–1780*, 216, 283, 425. Johnson, *Traditions and Reminiscences*, 134–37. Johnson, *Sketches of the Life and Correspondence of Nathanael Greene*, 1:268–69, 279.

30. Wallace, *The History of South Carolina*, 2:168. McCrady, *The History of South Carolina in the Revolution, 1775–1780*, 177–81, 208, 212.

31. McCrady, *The History of South Carolina in the Revolution, 1775–1780*, 266–74.

32. Ibid., 207. Howe, *History of the Presbyterian Church in South Carolina*, 1:370. Wallace, *The History of South Carolina*, 2:169–70.

33. Lambert, *South Carolina Loyalists in the American Revolution*, 59–69. Wallace, *The History of South Carolina*, 2:180. McCrady, *The History of South Carolina in the Revolution, 1775–1780*, 266–74.

34. Moss, *Roster of South Carolina Patriots in the American Revolution*, 80, 761, 803, et passim. McCrady, *The History of South Carolina in the Revolution, 1775–1780*, 286–87, 333–42, 354, 379, 385, 395. National Archives "Pension and Bounty-Land Warrant Application Files Based on Revolutionary War Service," microcopy M804, roll 1902, file S21417, application of Alexander Peden, South Carolina Line.

35. McCrady, *The History of South Carolina in the Revolution, 1775–1780*, 62–64, 333–42, 354, 379, 385, 395.

36. Wallace, *The History of South Carolina*, 2:176–77. McCrady, *The History of South Carolina in the Revolution, 1775–1780*, 298–303, 341, 401.

37. McCrady, *The History of South Carolina in the Revolution, 1775–1780*, 335–36, 341–42, 401.

38. Pope, *The History of Newberry County*, 1:46. Lambert, *South Carolina Loyalists in the American Revolution*, 69–74.

39. Lambert, *South Carolina Loyalists in the American Revolution*, 74.

40. Bailey and Cooper, *Biographical Directory of the South Carolina House of Representatives*, 3:29–30. Moss, *Roster of South Carolina Patriots in the American Revolution*, 841. McCrady, *The History of South Carolina in the Revolution, 1775–1780*, 320–29. Lambert, *South Carolina Loyalists in the American Revolution*, 81–84.

41. McCrady, *The History of South Carolina in the Revolution, 1775–1780*, 339. Wallace, *The History of South Carolina*, 2:187. Lawrence S. Rowland,

Alexander Moore, and George C. Rogers Jr., *The History of Beaufort County, South Carolina, vol. 1, 1514–1861* (Columbia: University of South Carolina Press, 1996), 215–20.

42. McCrady, *The History of South Carolina in the Revolution, 1775–1780*, 354. Wallace, *The History of South Carolina*, 2:186–89.

43. David B. Mattern, *Benjamin Lincoln and the American Revolution* (Columbia: University of South Carolina Press, 1995), 69–71. McCrady, *The History of South Carolina in the Revolution, 1775–1780*, 352–56. Wallace, *The History of South Carolina*, 2:187–89. Lambert, *South Carolina Loyalists in the American Revolution*, 85–88.

44. McCrady, *The History of South Carolina in the Revolution, 1775–1780*, 360–75. Wallace, *The History of South Carolina*, 2:189–92.

45. Mattern, *Benjamin Lincoln and the American Revolution*, 70–71. Wallace, *The History of South Carolina*, 2:192–93. McCrady, *The History of South Carolina in the Revolution, 1775–1780*, 392–94.

46. Wallace, *The History of South Carolina*, 2:192–93. McCrady, *The History of South Carolina in the Revolution, 1775–1780*, 396–97.

47. Wallace, *The History of South Carolina*, 2:192–93. McCrady, *The History of South Carolina in the Revolution, 1775–1780*, 392–94. Rowland, Moore, and Rogers, *The History of Beaufort County, South Carolina*, 222–28. Fraser, *Charleston! Charleston!*, 157–58. Lambert, *South Carolina Loyalists in the American Revolution*, 86–87.

THREE

1. Rowland, Moore, and Rogers, *The History of Beaufort County*, 226–28.

2. Ibid., 228–30. Higginbotham, *War of American Independence*, 355. Lumpkin, *From Savannah to Yorktown*, 33–40. McCrady, *The History of South Carolina in the Revolution, 1775–1780*, 404–19.

3. Henry Clinton, *The American Rebellion: Sir Henry Clinton's Narrative of His Campaigns, 1775–1782, with an Appendix of Original Documents*, William B. Willcox, ed. (New Haven, CT: Yale University Press, 1954), 151. Lambert, *South Carolina Loyalists in the American Revolution*, 94–95. Weigley, *The Partisan War*, 8.

4. Clinton, *The American Rebellion*, 158–60. Lumpkin, *From Savannah to Yorktown*, 41–42.

5. McCrady, *The History of South Carolina in the Revolution, 1775–1780*, 445–46.

6. Ibid., 449. Clinton, *The American Rebellion*, 157–72. George Smith McCowen Jr., *The British Occupation of Charleston, 1780–1782*, Tricentennial Studies 5, published for the South Carolina Tricentennial Commission (Columbia: University of South Carolina Press, 1972), 5.

7. Thomas Cooper and David J. McCord, eds., *The Statutes at Large of South*

Carolina, 10 vols. (Columbia: A.S. Johnston, 1838–41), 4:505. Edgar, *South Carolina*, 233.

8. McCrady, *The History of South Carolina in the Revolution, 1775–1780*, 471–79. Lumpkin, *From Savannah to Yorktown*, 47–49. Mattern, *Benjamin Lincoln and the American Revolution*, 97–109. McCowen, *The British Occupation of Charleston*, 7–9; Moultrie quote, 8.

9. Wickwire and Wickwire, *Cornwallis*, 205. Clinton, *The American Rebellion*, 166. Buchanan, *The Road to Guilford Courthouse*, 60–64. McCrady, *The History of South Carolina in the Revolution, 1775–1780*, 468–70. Charles Stedman, *History of the Origin, Progress, and Termination of the American War*, 2 vols. (London: J. Murray, 1794), 2:203–4. Lambert, *South Carolina Loyalists in the American Revolution*, 99. Christopher Hibbert, *Redcoats and Rebels: The American Revolution Through British Eyes* (New York: W. W. Norton & Co., 1990), 265–66.

10. There is some debate about how many men remained in Lincoln's army in May 1780. Older sources, such as McCrady and Wallace, place the figure at between 5,100 and 5,700. More recent writers, such as Buchanan, give a much lower figure of fewer than 3,400. McCrady, *The History of South Carolina in the Revolution, 1775–1780*, 507–8. Wallace, *The History of South Carolina*, 2:201. Weigley, *The Partisan War*, 8. Mattern, *Benjamin Lincoln and the American Revolution*, 97–109.

11. *Royal Gazette* quoted in Benjamin Franklin Hough, *The Siege of Charleston, by the British Fleet and Army Under the Command of Admiral Arbuthnot and Sir Henry Clinton* (Albany, NY: J. Hunsell, 1867), 172. McCowen, *The British Occupation of Charleston*, 9–10. McCrady, *The History of South Carolina in the Revolution, 1775–1780*, 514.

12. William Moultrie, *Memoirs of the American Revolution, So Far as It Is Related to the States of North and South Carolina, and Georgia*, 2 vols. (New York: David Longworth, 1802), 2:106–7.

13. McCowen, *The British Occupation of Charleston*, 44–47; Simpson quote, 46, 47.

14. McCrady, *The History of South Carolina in the Revolution, 1775–1780*, 525. Lambert, *South Carolina Loyalists in the American Revolution*, 106–7. Gregorie, *Thomas Sumter*, 76–77. Landrum, *Colonial and Revolutionary History of Upper South Carolina*, 104.

15. McCowen, *The British Occupation of Charleston*, 9.

16. Buchanan, *The Road to Guilford Courthouse*, 80. Address of Georgetown citizens quoted in George C. Rogers Jr., *The History of Georgetown County, South Carolina* (Columbia: University of South Carolina Press, 1970), 123.

17. A. S. Salley Jr., ed., *Colonel William Hill's Memoirs of the Revolution*, printed for the Historical Commission of South Carolina (Columbia: State Co., 1921), 7. McCrady, *The History of South Carolina in the Revolution*,

1775–1780, 533–35. Gregorie, *Thomas Sumter*, 77. Landrum, *Colonial and Revolutionary History of Upper South Carolina*, 105–6.

18. Clinton quoted in Banastre Tarleton, *A History of the Campaigns of 1780 and 1781, in the Southern Provinces of North America* (London: T. Caddell in the Strand, 1787), 80.

19. McCrady, *The History of South Carolina in the Revolution, 1775–1780*, 533–35. Clinton, *The American Rebellion*, 181. McCowen, *The British Occupation of Charleston*, 11. Stedman, *History of the Origins, Progress, and Termination of the American War*, 2:352.

20. Clinton, *The American Rebellion*, 181. McCrady, *The History of South Carolina in the Revolution, 1775–1780*, 533–35. McCowen, *The British Occupation of Charleston*, 52–54. Calhoon, *Loyalists in Revolutionary America*, 486.

21. Clinton, *The American Rebellion*, 181. Stedman, *History of the Origins, Progress, and Termination of the American War*, 2:220–21.

22. Stedman, *History of the Origins, Progress, and Termination of the American War*, 2:220–21.

23. Buchanan, *The Road to Guilford Courthouse*, 80–82. McCrady, *The History of South Carolina in the Revolution, 1775–1780*, 519.

24. McCrady, *The History of South Carolina in the Revolution, 1775–1780*, 518–19. Buchanan, *The Road to Guilford Courthouse*, 82.

25. Tarleton, *History of the Campaigns of 1780 and 1781, in the Southern Provinces of North America*, 29–31. Buchanan, *The Road to Guilford Courthouse*, 84–85. McCrady, *The History of South Carolina in the Revolution, 1775–1780*, 519–24. Lambert, *South Carolina Loyalists in the American Revolution*, 99. Nadelhaft, *The Disorders of War*, 57.

26. Howe, *History of the Presbyterian Church in South Carolina*, 1:536–37. James, *The Life of Andrew Jackson*, 19. Sam Thomas, *The Dye Is Cast: The Scots-Irish and Revolution in the Carolina Backcountry* (Columbia, SC: Palmetto Conservation Foundation, 1997), 16.

27. Howe, *History of the Presbyterian Church in South Carolina*, 1:536–37, 539. Remini, *Andrew Jackson and the Course of American Empire*, 14–15. Buchanan, *The Road to Guilford Courthouse*, 85, 88–89. Moss, *The Old Iron District*, 56–57. Gregorie, *Thomas Sumter*, 76–77. Robert D. Bass, *Gamecock: The Life and Campaigns of General Thomas Sumter* (New York: Holt, Reinhart and Winston, 1961), 53. Thomas, *The Dye Is Cast*, 16–17.

28. Salley, *Colonel William Hill's Memoirs of the Revolution*, 6–7; quote, 7.

29. Ibid., 7–8. McCrady, *The History of South Carolina in the Revolution, 1775–1780*, 588–90. Bass, *Gamecock*, 54. FitzHugh McMaster, *History of Fairfield County, South Carolina from "Before the White Man Came" to 1942* (Columbia: State Commercial Printing Co., 1946), 24. Buchanan, *The Road to Guilford Courthouse*, 111–12.

30. McCrady, *The History of South Carolina in the Revolution, 1775–1780*, 590. Bass, *Gamecock*, 54.

31. Turnbull quoted in Buchanan, *The Road to Guilford Courthouse*, 112.

32. Howe, *History of the Presbyterian Church in South Carolina*, 1:424–26, 509. There were actually two separate churches called Fishing Creek. The original congregation was founded in the early 1750s. In 1771, when a second church was formed, the original congregation was called Lower Fishing Creek and the new one Upper Fishing Creek. Simpson was the pastor of both congregations. Howe, *History of the Presbyterian Church in South Carolina*, 1:424.

33. McCrady, *The History of South Carolina in the Revolution, 1775–1780*, 591–92. Howe, *History of the Presbyterian Church in South Carolina*, 1: 511–13. Bass, *Gamecock*, 55.

34. Salley, *Colonel William Hill's Memoirs of the Revolution*, 8. Bass, *Gamecock*, 54–55. McCrady, *The History of South Carolina in the Revolution, 1775–1780*, 592–93. Lambert, *South Carolina Loyalists in the American Revolution*, 126. Gregorie, *Thomas Sumter*, 78.

35. Cornwallis quoted in Tarleton, *History of the Campaigns of 1780 and 1781, in the Southern Provinces of North America*, 117.

36. Rogers, *The History of Georgetown County, South Carolina*, 124–25.

37. Lambert, *South Carolina Loyalists in the American Revolution*, 112. Pope, *The History of Newberry County, South Carolina*, 1:47. Rogers, *The History of Georgetown County, South Carolina*, 124–25.

38. Rogers, *The History of Georgetown County, South Carolina*, 125–26. Lambert, *Loyalists in South Carolina in the American Revolution*, 115–16.

39. Wickwire and Wickwire, *Cornwallis*, 175–76; Cornwallis quote, 175. Bass, *Gamecock*, 54.

40. Gregorie, *Thomas Sumter*, 74–75. Bass, *Gamecock*, 22, 51–52.

41. Howe, *History of the Presbyterian Church in South Carolina*, 1: 412, 489, 581. McCrady, *The History of South Carolina in the Revolution, 1775–1780*, 747–48. Buchanan, *The Road to Guilford Courthouse*, 185. Ramsay, *History of South Carolina*, 1:217. Nadelhaft, *The Disorders of War*, 57–58; Kinloch quote, 58.

42. Rogers, *The History of Georgetown County, South Carolina*, 122. Stedman, *History of the Origin, Progress, and Termination of the American War*, 2:215, 220, 229; quote, 215.

43. Lambert, *South Carolina Loyalists in the American Revolution*, 115. Ramsay, *History of South Carolina*, 1:235.

44. Gregorie, *Thomas Sumter*, 74–75; William Dobein James, *A Sketch of the Life of Brig. Gen. Francis Marion, and a History of His Brigade . . .* (Charleston, SC: n.p., 1821), quote, 75.

45. James Potter Collins, *Autobiography of a Revolutionary Soldier*, ed. John M. Roberts (1839; reprint, New York: Arno Press, 1979), 24–25.

46. Collins, *A Goodly Heritage*, 48.

47. Howe, *History of the Presbyterian Church in South Carolina*, 1:500. [Elizabeth Fries Lummis] Ellet, *Domestic History of the American Revolution* (New

York: Baker and Scribner, 1850), 175–79. Glasgow Melancthon Williams, *History of the Reformed Presbyterian Church in America* (Baltimore: Hill & Harvey, 1888), 380–84.

48. Ellet, *Domestic History of the Revolution*, 179.
49. Ibid., 180.
50. Ibid., 181–82. Moss, *Roster of South Carolina Patriots in the American Revolution*, 21.
51. Ellet, *Domestic History of the American Revolution*, 182. Collins, *A Goodly Heritage*, 48. Howe, *History of the Presbyterian Church in South Carolina*, 1:500–501. Ulmer, *The Covenanters of Chester County*, 2. Ulmer, *The Covenanters of Fairfield County*, 5.
52. Nadelhaft, *The Disorders of War*, 55–60. Clinton quoted in Rogers, *The History of Georgetown County, South Carolina*, 125.
53. Klein, *Unification of a Slave State*, 80, 84–85. Ramsay, *History of South Carolina*, 1:193. Nadelhaft, *The Disorders of War*, 55–60. Weigley, *The Partisan War*, 13–15. Higginbotham, *War of American Independence*, 360–64.

FOUR

1. Ramsay, *History of South Carolina*, 1:199. Bass, *Gamecock*, 52–54. Gregorie, *Thomas Sumter*, 78–82.
2. Ibid. Turnbull quoted in Hampton Jarrell, "Huck's Defeat: A Turning of the Tide" (unpublished manuscript, Historical Center of York County, York, SC), 1–2. McCrady, *The History of South Carolina in the Revolution, 1775–1780*, 592–93.
3. McCrady, *The History of South Carolina in the Revolution, 1775–1780*, 533–35.
4. Samuel C. Williams, ed., "General Winn's Notes—1780," *South Carolina Historical and Genealogical Magazine* 43 (1942): 207.
5. Bass, *Gamecock*, 53–56; quote, 56. Gregorie, *Thomas Sumter*, 80. Ramsay, *History of South Carolina*, 199.
6. Bass, *Gamecock*, 55–56. Williams, "General Winn's Notes—1780," 206–7.
7. James Williams's letter in Gibbes, *Documentary History of the American Revolution*, 3:115–16. Moss, *South Carolina Patriots in the American Revolution*, 3, 803.
8. Blackwell P. Robinson, *William R. Davie* (Chapel Hill: University of North Carolina Press, 1959), 16–41.
9. Collins, *A Goodly Heritage*, 55. Moss, *South Carolina Patriots in the American Revolution*, 3, 28, 80, 96, 110, 126, 150, 151, 152, 161, 242, 347, 356–57, 411, 467, 494, 547, 606, 620, 694, 698, 803, 841. *Proceedings of a Celebration of Huck's Defeat at Brattonsville, York District, S.C., July 12th, 1839* (1839; reprint, Yorkville, SC, n.p., 1895), 9–12.
10. Quotation from a proclamation by Sir Henry Clinton, 22 May 1780, in Tar-

leton, *A History of the Campaigns of 1780 and 1781, in the Southern Provinces of North America*, 71. Ellet, *Domestic History of the Revolution*, 180.

11. Collins, *A Goodly Heritage*, 48.

12. James Williams's letter in Gibbes, *Documentary History of the American Revolution*, 2:135–37. Moss, *South Carolina Patriots in the American Revolution*, 995.

13. Bass, *Gamecock*, 56–58.

14. Lambert, *South Carolina Loyalists in the American Revolution*, 128.

15. Weigley, *The Partisan War*, 13. Klein, *Unification of a Slave State*, 78–108. Lambert, *South Carolina Loyalists in the American Revolution*, 104–16. Klein, "Frontier Planters and the American Revolution," 63. McCrady, *The History of South Carolina in the Revolution, 1775–1780*, 559–60.

16. George Park quoted in Klein, *Unification of a Slave State*, 100.

17. Brown, *The South Carolina Regulators*, 124. Klein, *Unification of a Slave State*, 78–108. Lambert, *South Carolina Loyalists in the American Revolution*, 17–18.

18. Brown, *The South Carolina Regulators*, 124. Klein, *Unification of a Slave State*, 78–108. Holman, "William Gilmore Simms' Picture of the Revolution as a Civil Conflict," 441–62. Ramsay, *History of South Carolina*, 1:259. Lambert, *South Carolina Loyalists in the American Revolution*, 17–18.

19. Lambert, *South Carolina Loyalists in the American Revolution*, 129. Tarleton, *History of the Campaigns of 1780 and 1781, in the Southern Provinces of North America*, 86, 121. Jarrell, "Huck's Defeat."

20. Turnbull's order quoted in Fairey, *Historic Brattonsville*, 13.

21. Huck's comments quoted in Salley, *Colonel William Hill's Memoirs of the Revolution*, 9; and Bailey, *Commanders at King's Mountain*, 203. McCrady, *The History of South Carolina in the Revolution, 1775–1780*, 588–90. Bass, *Gamecock*, 54–55. Ramsay, *History of South Carolina*, 1:201. Collins, *Autobiography of a Revolutionary Soldier*, 24–25.

22. Weigley, *The Partisan War*, 13–14. Salley, *Colonel William Hill's Memoirs of the Revolution* 9; McCrady, *The History of South Carolina in the Revolution, 1775–1780*, 588–90. Bass, *Gamecock*, 54–55. Ramsay, *History of South Carolina*, 1:201.

23. Bailey, *Commanders at King's Mountain*, 204. Ellet, *Domestic History of the Revolution*, 192. Elizabeth F. Ellet, "Heroic Women of the Revolution: Martha Bratton," *Godey's Magazine* (June 1848): 245. John J. Kleber, *The Kentucky Encyclopedia* (Lexington: University Press of Kentucky, 1992), 1.

24. Wickwire and Wickwire, *Cornwallis*, 170–75. Fairey, *Historic Brattonsville*, 11. Thomas, "The 1780 Presbyterian Rebellion and the Battle of Huck's Defeat," passim. Ellet, *Domestic History of the Revolution*, 193.

25. Wickwire and Wickwire, *Cornwallis*, 170. Tarleton, *History of the Campaigns of 1780 and 1781, in the Southern Provinces of North America*, 85. Fairey, *Historic Brattonsville*, 11.

26. McCrady, *The History of South Carolina in the Revolution, 1775–1780*, 594.

Bailey, *Commanders at King's Mountain*, 202–3. Ellet, *Domestic History of the Revolution*, 189–90. Fairey, *Historic Brattonsville*, 14.

27. McCrady, *The History of South Carolina in the Revolution, 1775–1780*, 594. Bailey, *Commanders at King's Mountain*, 202–3. Ellet, *Domestic History of the Revolution*, 190. Fairey, *Historic Brattonsville*, 14.

28. Fairey, *Historic Brattonsville*, 14. Bailey, *Commanders at King's Mountain*, 202–3.

29. Thomas J. Kirkland and Robert M. Kennedy, *Historic Camden, Part One: Colonial and Revolutionary* (Columbia, SC: The State Company, 1905), 281–82. Ellet, *Heroic Women of the Revolution*, 240–42. Bailey, *Commanders at King's Mountain*, 205–6. Ellet, *Domestic History of the Revolution*, 192.

30. Kirkland and Kennedy, *Historic Camden*, 281–82. Ellet, *Heroic Women of the Revolution*, 240–42. Bailey, *Commanders at King's Mountain*, 205–6. Ellet, *Domestic History of the Revolution*, 192. Fairey, *Historic Brattonsville*, 14.

31. Kirkland and Kennedy, *Historic Camden*, 282. Fairey, *Historic Brattonsville*, 14.

32. M. A. Moore Sr., *The Life of General Edward Lacey* (Spartanburg, SC: Douglas, Evins & Co., 1859), 10n. Fairey, *Historic Brattonsville*, 14–15. Bailey, *Commanders at King's Mountain*, 206. Kirkland and Kennedy, *Historic Camden*, 282. Ellet, *Historic Women of the Revolution*, 242. *Proceedings of a Celebration of Huck's Defeat*, 5.

33. Tarleton, *History of the Campaigns of 1780 and 1781, in the Southern Provinces of North America*, 121. Fairey, *Historic Brattonsville*, 14–15. Kirkland and Kennedy, *Historic Camden*, 282. Ellet, *Historic Women of the Revolution*, 242. Bailey, *Commanders at King's Mountain*, 208. Moore, *The Life of General Edward Lacey*, 10n. Johnson, *Traditions and Reminiscences of the American Revolution in the South*, 338.

34. Fairey, *Historic Brattonsville*, 14.

35. Ibid., 15–16.

36. Tarleton, *History of the Campaigns of 1780 and 1781, in the Southern Provinces of North America*, 93; Cornwallis quote, 121. Fairey, *Historic Brattonsville*, 15–16. Buchanan, *The Road to Guilford Courthouse*, 113. Williams, "General Winn's Notes—1780," 205.

37. Buchanan, *The Road to Guilford Courthouse*, 114. McCrady, *The History of South Carolina in the Revolution*, 594.

38. Moore, *The Life of General Edward Lacey*, 7–8. McCrady, *The History of South Carolina in the Revolution*, 595.

39. Moore, *The Life of General Edward Lacey*, 9. Buchanan, *The Road to Guilford Courthouse*, 114. McCrady, *The History of South Carolina in the Revolution, 1775–1780*, 594–96. Thomas, *The Dye Is Cast*, 21.

40. Moore, *The Life of General Edward Lacey*, 8. McCrady, *The History of South Carolina in the Revolution, 1775–1780*, 595–96.

41. Moore, *The Life of General Edward Lacey*, 8–9.
42. Johnson, *Traditions and Reminiscences of the American Revolution in the South*, 336–37. McCrady, *The History of South Carolina in the Revolution, 1775–1780*, 597. Bailey, *Commanders at King's Mountain*, 206–7.
43. Moore, *The Life of General Edward Lacey*, 8–9. Collins, *Autobiography of a Revolutionary Soldier*, 25–27. Moss, *South Carolina Patriots in the American Revolution*, 690.
44. Collins, *Autobiography of a Revolutionary Soldier*, 25–26. Moore, *The Life of General Edward Lacey*, 9–10. McCrady, *The History of South Carolina in the Revolution, 1775–1780*, 596–97. Salley, *Colonel William Hill's Memoirs of the Revolution*, 9–10. Thomas, *The Dye Is Cast*, 21–22.
45. Collins, *Autobiography of a Revolutionary Soldier*, 25.
46. Moore, *The Life of General Edward Lacey*, 9–10. Salley, *Colonel William Hill's Memoirs of the Revolution*, 10. Buchanan, *The Road to Guilford Courthouse*, 113–15. Lyman C. Draper, *King's Mountain and Its Heroes: History of the Battle of King's Mountain, October 7th, 1780 and the Events Which Led to It* (Cincinnati: P.G. Thomson, 1881), 500.
47. Ibid.
48. Moore, *The Life of General Edward Lacey*, 9–11. Salley, *Colonel William Hill's Memoirs of the Revolution*, 10. Buchanan, *The Road to Guilford Courthouse*, 113–15.
49. Bailey, *Commanders at King's Mountain*, 207–8. Moore, *The Life of General Edward Lacey*, 10.
50. Williams, "General Winn's Notes—1780," 206–7. Salley, *Colonel William Hill's Memoirs of the Revolution*, 10. Moore, *The Life of General Edward Lacey*, 10. Buchanan, *The Road to Guilford Courthouse*, 114–15.
51. Lumpkin, *From Savannah to Yorktown*, 83. Fairey, *Historic Brattonsville*, 16. Thomas, "The 1780 Presbyterian Rebellion and the Battle of Huck's Defeat."
52. McCrady, *The History of South Carolina in the Revolution, 1775–1780*, 598. Kirkland and Kennedy, *Historic Camden*, 283.
53. Johnson, *Traditions and Reminiscences of the American Revolution in the South*, 338–39. Ellet, *Heroic Women of the Revolution*, 244.
54. Kirkland and Kennedy, *Historic Camden*, 283. Moss, *South Carolina Patriots in the American Revolution*, 161.
55. Kirkland and Kennedy, *Historic Camden*, 283–84.
56. Ibid., 281–90. Johnson, *Traditions and Reminiscences of the American Revolution in the South*, 339.
57. Ellet, *Heroic Women of the Revolution*, 245–46.
58. McCrady, *The History of South Carolina in the Revolution, 1775–1780*, 599. Buchanan, *The Road to Guilford Courthouse*, 115.
59. Bancroft, *History of the United States*, 10:313. Johnson, *Traditions and Remi-*

niscences of the Revolution, 339. Lumpkin, *From Savannah to Yorktown*, 83. Salley, *Colonel William Hill's Memoirs of the Revolution*, 10.

60. Johnson, *Traditions and Reminiscences of the Revolution*, 339. Buchanan, *The Road to Guilford Courthouse*, 131–32. Lumpkin, *From Savannah to Yorktown*, 83. Lambert, *South Carolina Loyalists in the American Revolution*, 128. Tarleton, *History of the Campaigns of 1780 and 1781, in the Southern Provinces of North America*, 93. Jarrell, "Huck's Defeat: A Turning of the Tide," 4.

61. Wickwire and Wickwire, *Cornwallis*, 191. Moore, *The Life of General Edward Lacey*, 11.

FIVE

1. Gregorie, *Thomas Sumter*, 85–86. Wickwire and Wickwire, *Cornwallis*, 135–37.

2. Buchanan, *The Road to Guilford Courthouse*, 115. Balfour quoted in Jarrell, "Huck's Defeat: A Turning of the Tide," 5. Wickwire and Wickwire, *Cornwallis*, 169–71. Lambert, *South Carolina Loyalists in the American Revolution*, 78–124.

3. Ferguson and Balfour quoted in Jarrell, "Huck's Defeat: A Turning of the Tide," 5.

4. Higginbotham, *War of American Independence*, 362. The remaining four engagements occurred in the swamps of the lowcountry where Francis Marion, the "Swamp Fox," was giving the British and Tories fits. Edward McCrady, *The History of South Carolina in the Revolution, 1780–1783* (New York: Macmillan, 1902), 744–47. Terry Lipscomb, *Battles, Skirmishes, and Actions of the American Revolution in South Carolina* (Columbia: South Carolina Department of Archives and History, 1991), passim.

5. Nadelhaft, *The Disorders of War*, 61. Jarrell, "Huck's Defeat: A Turning of the Tide," 4–6. Lumpkin, *From Savannah to Yorktown*, 83.

6. McCrady, *The History of South Carolina in the Revolution, 1775–1780*, 600–601. Johnson, *Traditions and Reminiscences of the American Revolution in the South*, 446–47. Buchanan, *The Road to Guilford Courthouse*, 104.

7. Simms, *Joscelyn*, 79. Johnson, *Traditions and Reminiscences of the American Revolution in the South*, 446–47.

8. Claude Henry Neuffer, *Names in South Carolina*, vols. 19–24 (1972–1978; reprint, Spartanburg, SC: Reprint Co., 1983), 22:35. Buchanan, *The Road to Guilford Courthouse*, 104–5. McCrady, *The History of South Carolina in the Revolution, 1775–1780*, 600–601.

9. McCrady, *The History of South Carolina in the Revolution, 1775–1780*, 601. Johnson, *Traditions and Reminiscences of the Revolution in the South*, 447. Buchanan, *The Road to Guilford Courthouse*, 105.

10. Johnson, *Traditions and Reminiscences of the Revolution in the South*, 447. Buchanan, *The Road to Guilford Courthouse*, 105.

11. Ibid.

12. Moss, *South Carolina Patriots in the American Revolution*, 925. Bailey and Cooper, *Biographical Directory of the South Carolina House of Representatives*, 3:708–9. McCrady, *The History of South Carolina in the Revolution, 1775–1780*, 608–9.

13. McCrady, *The History of South Carolina in the Revolution, 1775–1780*, 608–9. Howe, *History of the Presbyterian Church in South Carolina*, 1:534. Draper, *King's Mountain and Its Heroes*, 73–75.

14. Landrum, *Colonial and Revolutionary History of Upper South Carolina*, 111–12. McCrady, *The History of South Carolina in the Revolution, 1775–1780*, 608–09. Howe, *History of the Presbyterian Church in South Carolina*, 1:534. Draper, *King's Mountain and Its Heroes*, 73–75, 79. Elizabeth F. Ellet, *The Women of the American Revolution*, 2 vols. (New York: Baker and Scribner, 1848), 1:250–62.

15. Draper, *King's Mountain and Its Heroes*, 79. Landrum, *Colonial and Revolutionary History of Upper South Carolina*, 116.

16. McCrady, *The History of South Carolina in the Revolution, 1775–1780*, 611–13. Draper, *King's Mountain and Its Heroes*, 78–79.

17. McCrady, *The History of South Carolina in the Revolution, 1775–1780*, 611–13. Landrum, *Colonial and Revolutionary History of Upper South Carolina*, 115–16.

18. Landrum, *Colonial and Revolutionary History of Upper South Carolina*, 116–17. Draper, *King's Mountain and Its Heroes*, 78–80. McCrady, *The History of South Carolina in the Revolution, 1775–1780*, 611–13.

19. Draper, *King's Mountain and Its Heroes*, 76.

20. Ibid., 80. Landrum, *Colonial and Revolutionary History of Upper South Carolina*, 118–20.

21. Draper, *King's Mountain and Its Heroes*, 79–80. Landrum, *Colonial and Revolutionary History of Upper South Carolina*, 120–22, 127. McCrady, *The History of South Carolina in the Revolution, 1775–1780*, 614–15.

22. McCrady, *The History of the Revolution in South Carolina, 1775–1780*, 614. Landrum, *Colonial and Revolutionary History of Upper South Carolina*, 114–15. Moss, *The Old Iron District*, 58.

23. Draper, *King's Mountain and Its Heroes*, 79–83. Landrum, *Colonial and Revolutionary History of Upper South Carolina*, 120–22. McCrady, *The History of South Carolina in the Revolution, 1775–1780*, 614–15.

24. Draper, *King's Mountain and Its Heroes*, 80–81. Landrum, *Colonial and Revolutionary History of Upper South Carolina*, 121–22. McCrady, *The History of South Carolina in the Revolution, 1775–1780*, 614–15.

25. McCrady, *The History of South Carolina in the Revolution, 1780–1783*,

746–47. Draper, *King's Mountain and Its Heroes*, 81–82. Landrum, *Colonial and Revolutionary History of Upper South Carolina*, 122–26. McCrady, *The History of South Carolina in the Revolution, 1775–1780*, 614–15.

26. Draper, *King's Mountain and Its Heroes*, 82–83. Landrum, *Colonial and Revolutionary History of Upper South Carolina*, 122–26. McCrady, *The History of South Carolina in the Revolution, 1775–1780*, 614–15.

27. Ibid.

28. Ibid. Howe, *History of the Presbyterian Church in South Carolina*, 1:542.

29. Landrum, *Colonial and Revolutionary History of Upper South Carolina*, 125–26.

30. Ibid., 126–27.

31. Robinson, *William R. Davie*, 44–45.

32. Ibid., 46.

33. Ibid., 46–47.

34. Moss, *The Old Iron District*, 58–59. Landrum, *Colonial and Revolutionary History of Upper South Carolina*, 130. McCrady, *The History of South Carolina in the Revolution, 1775–1780*, 634. Draper, *King's Mountain and Its Heroes*, 89.

35. Moss, *The Old Iron District*, 59. Moss, *Roster of South Carolina Patriots in the American Revolution*, 496. Landrum, *Colonial and Revolutionary History of Upper South Carolina*, 131. Draper, *King's Mountain and Its Heroes*, 86–87.

36. Landrum, *Colonial and Revolutionary History of Upper South Carolina*, 131.

37. Ibid., 114–15, 132–33.

38. McCrady, *The History of South Carolina in the Revolution, 1775–1780*, 634–35. Moss, *The Old Iron District*, 59–60. Landrum, *Colonial and Revolutionary History of Upper South Carolina*, 133–34. Works Projects Administration, *A History of Spartanburg County*, 26–27. Draper, *King's Mountain and Its Heroes*, 88–89.

39. Landrum, *Colonial and Revolutionary History of Upper South Carolina*, 133–34. Moss, *The Old Iron District*, 59–60. Draper, *King's Mountain and Its Heroes*, 88–89.

40. Landrum, *Colonial and Revolutionary History of Upper South Carolina*, 133–34. McCrady, *The History of South Carolina in the Revolution, 1775–1780*, 634–35. Works Projects Administration, *A History of Spartanburg County*, 26–27.

41. Landrum, *Colonial and Revolutionary History of Upper South Carolina*, 133–34. Works Projects Administration, *A History of Spartanburg County*, 26–27.

42. McCrady, *The History of South Carolina in the Revolution, 1775–1780*, 623–24. Bass, *Gamecock*, 63–64.

43. McCrady, *The History of South Carolina in the Revolution, 1775–1780*, 624. Buchanan, *The Road to Guilford Courthouse*, 131–32. Gregorie, *Thomas Sumter*, 86–88. Bass, *Gamecock*, 65. Salley, *Colonel William Hill's Memoirs of the Revolution*, 11.

44. Turnbull quoted in Bass, *Gamecock*, 65. Salley, *Colonel William Hill's Memoirs of the Revolution*, 11. Buchanan, *The Road to Guilford Courthouse*, 133. Bass, *Gamecock*, 65.

45. Salley, *Colonel William Hill's Memoirs of the American Revolution*, 11–12. Buchanan, *The Road to Guilford Courthouse*, 132–33.

46. Buchanan, *The Road to Guilford Courthouse*, 132.

47. McCrady, *The History of South Carolina in the Revolution, 1775–1780*, 625. Buchanan, *The Road to Guilford Courthouse*, 133.

48. Ibid. Blackwell P. Robinson, ed., *The Revolutionary War Sketches of William R. Davie*, North Carolina Bicentennial Pamphlet Series, *North Carolina in the American Revolution*, Jeffrey J. Crow, ed. (Raleigh: North Carolina Department of Cultural Resources, Division of Archives and History, 1976), 12.

49. Robinson, *William R. Davie*, 50. Bass, *Gamecock*, 68.

50. Ibid. Robinson, *The Revolutionary War Sketches of William R. Davie*, 13. Buchanan, *The Road to Guilford Courthouse*, 133.

51. Robinson, *The Revolutionary War Sketches of William R. Davie*, 14. Buchanan, *The Road to Guilford Courthouse*, 135. Robinson, *William R. Davie*, 51–53. Bass, *Gamecock*, 68–70. Gregorie, *Thomas Sumter*, 92–94.

52. Robinson, *The Revolutionary War Sketches of William R. Davie*, 14. Robinson, *William R. Davie*, 52–53. Buchanan, *The Road to Guilford Courthouse*, 135. Bass, *Gamecock*, 69–70.

53. Robinson, *William R. Davie*, 52–53. Buchanan, *The Road to Guilford Courthouse*, 135–36. Bass, *Gamecock*, 69–70.

54. Robinson, *The Revolutionary War Sketches of William R. Davie*, 15. Robinson, *William R. Davie*, 52–53. Buchanan, *The Road to Guilford Courthouse*, 135–36. Bass, *Gamecock*, 69–70. Remini, *Andrew Jackson and the Course of American Empire*, 17.

55. Salley, *Colonel William Hill's Memoirs of the Revolution*, 13. Buchanan, *The Road to Guilford Courthouse*, 135–36.

56. Landrum, *Colonial and Revolutionary History of Upper South Carolina*, 135–46. Buchanan, *The Road to Guilford Courthouse*, 137–41. Draper, *King's Mountain and Its Heroes*, 89–102. McCrady, *The History of the Revolution in South Carolina, 1775–1780*, 635–40.

57. Buchanan, *The Road to Guilford Courthouse*, 142–51.

58. Ibid., 153–55; quote, 154 (from William Seymour, *A Journal of the Southern Expedition, 1780–1783*).

59. Higginbotham, *War of American Independence*, 358–59. Weigley, *The Partisan War*, 19–20. McCrady, *The History of South Carolina in the Revolution, 1775–1780*, 655–66.

60. Bass, *Gamecock*, 78–79. Gregorie, *Thomas Sumter*, 98–99.

61. Weigley, *The Partisan War*, 19. Buchanan, *The Road to Guilford Courthouse*,

155. McCrady, *The History of South Carolina in the Revolution, 1775–1780*, 649.

62. Bass, *Gamecock*, 78–79.

63. Ibid., 79. Buchanan, *The Road to Guilford Courthouse*, 136–37.

64. Weigley, *The Partisan War*, 19–21; quote, 20.

65. Ibid., 19–21.

66. Wickwire and Wickwire, *Cornwallis*, 162–63. Buchanan, *The Road to Guilford Courthouse*, 168–69.

67. Higginbotham, *War of American Independence*, 359–60. McCrady, *The History of South Carolina in the Revolution, 1775–1780*, 669–80. Weigley, *The Partisan War*, 19–21. Buchanan, *The Road to Guilford Courthouse*, 157–72.

68. Stedman, *History of the Origin, Progress, and Termination of the American War*, 2:210.

69. Buchanan, *The Road to Guilford Courthouse*, 169–70. Wickwire and Wickwire, *Cornwallis*, 163–64. Weigley, *The Partisan War*, 21.

70. McCrady, *The History of South Carolina in the Revolution, 1775–1780*, 680–81. Robinson, *William R. Davie*, 58–59. Buchanan, *The Road to Guilford Courthouse*, 173.

71. McCrady, *The History of South Carolina in the Revolution, 1775–1780*, 681–82. Buchanan, *The Road to Guilford Courthouse*, 173–74. Tarleton, *History of the Campaigns of 1780 and 1781, in the Southern Provinces of North America*, 111–13.

72. Buchanan, *The Road to Guilford Courthouse*, 174–75. McCrady, *The History of the Revolution in South Carolina, 1775–1780*, 682–83. Bass, *Gamecock*, 82–84. Gregorie, *Thomas Sumter*, 101–2.

73. Tarleton, *History of the Campaigns of 1780 and 1781, in the Southern Provinces of North America*, 113–15; quote, 114. Bass, *Gamecock*, 83–85. Gregorie, *Thomas Sumter*, 101–2.

74. Bass, *Gamecock*, 83–85; quote, 84. Tarleton, *History of the Campaigns of 1780 and 1781, in the Southern Provinces of North America*, 113–15. Robinson, *William R. Davie*, 59–60. Gregorie, *Thomas Sumter*, 101–2. Buchanan, *The Road to Guilford Courthouse*, 174–76. McCrady, *The History of the Revolution in South Carolina, 1775–1780*, 683–84.

75. Wickwire and Wickwire, *Cornwallis*, 163–65; Cornwallis quote, 165. Tarleton, *History of the Campaigns of 1780 and 1781, in the Southern Provinces of North America*, 156. Weigley, *The Partisan War*, 21.

76. Wickwire and Wickwire, *Cornwallis*, 192–93. Cornwallis quote, 193.

77. Ibid., 194–95. Tarleton, *History of the Campaigns of 1780 and 1781, in the Southern Provinces of North America*, 155–56.

78. McCrady, *The History of the Revolution in South Carolina, 1775–1780*, 691–93; quote, 693.

79. Buchanan, *The Road to Guilford Courthouse*, 176–80. Works Projects Administration, *A History of Spartanburg County*, 27–28. Landrum, *Colonial and*

Revolutionary History of Upper South Carolina, 147–66. Draper, *King's Mountain and Its Heroes*, 103–22.

80. Bass, *Gamecock*, 84–101; Cornwallis quote, 85; Gates quote, 85. McCrady, *The History of South Carolina in the Revolution, 1775–1780*, 747–54.

81. Buchanan, *The Road to Guilford Courthouse*, 186–91. McCrady, *The History of South Carolina in the Revolution, 1775–1780*, 741–47.

82. Wickwire and Wickwire, *Cornwallis*, 208–9. Buchanan, *The Road to Guilford Courthouse*, 208–214; Ferguson quote, 208; Doak quote, 213.

83. Draper, *King's Mountain and Its Heroes*, 204. Buchanan, *The Road to Guilford Courthouse*, 218–19.

84. Buchanan, *The Road to Guilford Courthouse*, 222–23. Wickwire and Wickwire, *Cornwallis*, 209–10. McCrady, *The History of South Carolina in the Revolution, 1775–1780*, 782–83.

85. Wickwire and Wickwire, *Cornwallis*, 211–12. McCrady, *The History of South Carolina in the Revolution, 1775–1780*, 782–87.

86. Wickwire and Wickwire, *Cornwallis*, 208–12. Ferguson quoted in Tarleton, *History of the Campaigns of 1780 and 1781, in the Southern Provinces of North America*, 193.

87. Wickwire and Wickwire, *Cornwallis*, 210–11; Ferguson quote, 211. McCrady, *The History of South Carolina in the Revolution, 1775–1780*, 781–82.

88. Wickwire and Wickwire, *Cornwallis*, 212–15. McCrady, *The History of South Carolina in the Revolution, 1775–1780*, 789–802.

89. Ibid. Buchanan, *The Road to Guilford Courthouse*, 225–35.

90. Wickwire and Wickwire, *Cornwallis*, 212–15; Collins quote, 215. McCrady, *The History of South Carolina in the Revolution, 1775–1780*, 789–802. Buchanan, *The Road to Guilford Courthouse*, 225–35. Salley, *Colonel William Hill's Memoirs of the Revolution*, 22–24.

91. Wickwire and Wickwire, *Cornwallis*, 214–15. McCrady, *The History of South Carolina in the Revolution, 1775–1780*, 798–801. Buchanan, *The Road to Guilford Courthouse*, 233–34.

92. Buchanan, *The Road to Guilford Courthouse*, 233–34. Tarleton, *History of the Campaigns of 1780 and 1781, in the Southern Provinces of North America*, 165. Urinating on a foe for whom you had contempt was well ingrained into the behavior patterns of the Over Mountain Men. During the Nullification Crisis of 1832–33, a Tennessean wrote to President Andrew Jackson that if he were given two weeks' notice he could gather enough men "to stand on Saluda Mountains and piss enough . . . to float the whole nullifying crew of South Carolina, into the Atlantic Ocean." Edgar, *South Carolina*, 336.

93. McCrady, *The History of South Carolina in the Revolution, 1775–1780*, 803. Buchanan, *The Road to Guilford Courthouse*, 235–36.

94. McCrady, *The History of South Carolina in the Revolution, 1775–1780*, 801–2.

Wickwire and Wickwire, *Cornwallis*, 217. Buchanan, *The Road to Guilford Courthouse*, 237.

95. McCrady, *The History of South Carolina in the Revolution, 1775–1780*, 804–5. Draper, *King's Mountain and Its Heroes*, 265–66. Ramsay, *History of South Carolina*, 1:219. Wickwire and Wickwire, *Cornwallis*, 217–19.

96. Stedman, *History of the Origin, Progress, and Termination of the American War*, 2:237, 246–47. Ramsay, *History of South Carolina*, 1:219. McCrady, *The History of South Carolina in the Revolution, 1775–1776*, 805.

97. Higginbotham, *War of American Independence*, 364. Stedman, *History of the Origin, Progress, and Termination of the American War*, 2:214.

SIX

1. Wickwire and Wickwire, *Cornwallis*, 178–80; Cornwallis quote, 179.

2. Cornwallis quoted in Wickwire and Wickwire, *Cornwallis*, 174 (emphasis added).

3. Greene and his aide (William Pierce) quoted in Nadelhaft, *The Disorders of War*, 60.

4. Lambert, *South Carolina Loyalists in the American Revolution*, 198–99.

5. William Gilmore Simms, *The Scout*, published for the Southern Studies Program, University of South Carolina (1854; reprint, Spartanburg, SC: Reprint Co., 1976), 29.

6. Lambert, *South Carolina Loyalists in the American Revolution*, 189. Stedman, *History of the Origins, Progress, and Termination of the American War*, 2:237.

7. Rogers, *The History of Georgetown County*, 128–31; Cornwallis quote, 129. Klein, *Unification of a Slave State*, 100–105.

8. Nadelhaft, *The Disorders of War*, 61–63; Hampton quote, 62.

9. Lumpkin, *From Savannah to Yorktown*, 52. Lambert, *South Carolina Loyalists in the American Revolution*, 206–10. Nadelhaft, *The Disorders of War*, 58–60.

10. Ramsay, *The History of South Carolina*, 1:234–35.

11. Buchanan, *The Road to Guilford Courthouse*, 249–51. Bass, *Gamecock*, 99. Gregorie, *Thomas Sumter*, 116–17.

12. Buchanan, *The Road to Guilford Courthouse*, 192. Klein, *Unification of a Slave State*, 82–91. Klein, "Frontier Planters and the American Revolution in the South Carolina Backcountry," 37–69.

13. Howe, *History of the Presbyterian Church in South Carolina*, 1:508–11. Buchanan, *The Road to Guilford Courthouse*, 111. Hooker, *The Carolina Backcountry on the Eve of the Revolution*, 240–41.

14. McCrady, *The History of South Carolina in the Revolution, 1775–1780*, 816–17; Richardson quote, 816–17.

15. Moore, *The Life of General Edward Lacey*, 3–6.

16. Bass, *Gamecock*, 59.

17. Gregorie, *Thomas Sumter*, 115; Cornwallis quote, 115. Buchanan, *The Road to Guilford Courthouse*, 249. Bass, *Gamecock*, 96–97. Wickwire and Wickwire, *Cornwallis*, 223–24. McCrady, *The History of South Carolina in the Revolution, 1775–1780*, 819–21.

18. Gregorie, *Thomas Sumter*, 116. Buchanan, *The Road to Guilford Courthouse*, 249–50. Bass, *Gamecock*, 98–99. Wickwire and Wickwire, *Cornwallis*, 223–24. McCrady, *The History of South Carolina in the Revolution, 1775–1780*, 822–23.

19. Gregorie, *Thomas Sumter*, 115–17. Buchanan, *The Road to Guilford Courthouse*, 250–51. Bass, *Gamecock*, 98.

20. Buchanan, *The Road to Guilford Courthouse*, 251–59. Tarleton, *History of the Campaigns in 1780 and 1781, in the Southern Provinces of North America*, 174–80. Wickwire and Wickwire, *Cornwallis*, 224–25. Bass, *Gamecock*, 102–11. Gregorie, *Thomas Sumter*, 120–24. McCrady, *The History of South Carolina in the Revolution, 1775–1780*, 827–30.

21. Buchanan, *The Road to Guilford Courthouse*, 251–59; Tarleton quote, 258. Bass, *Gamecock*, 102–11. Gregorie, *Thomas Sumter*, 120–24. Cornwallis to Tarleton, 23 November 1780, in Tarleton, *History of the Campaigns of 1780 and 1781, in the Southern Provinces of British North America*, 203.

22. Nadelhaft, *Disorders of War*, 60; quote, 60.

23. Cornwallis quoted in Nadelhaft, *The Disorders of War*, 57, 60. McCrady, *The History of South Carolina in the Revolution, 1775–1780*, 710–11. Buchanan, *The Road to Guilford Courthouse*, 192.

24. Lambert, *South Carolina Loyalists in the American Revolution*, 200. Lumpkin, *From Savannah to Yorktown*, 74. Buchanan, *The Road to Guilford Courthouse*, 302. McCrady, *The History of South Carolina in the American Revolution, 1780–1783*, 473–75.

25. Huff, *Greenville*, 27–28; Bates quote, 28.

26. Simms, *The Partisan*, 53–55, 83–93; quote, 55. Holman, "William Gilmore Simms' Picture of the Revolution as a Civil Conflict," 451.

27. Amos Kendall (*The Life of Andrew Jackson*) quoted in Remini, *Andrew Jackson and the Course of American Empire*, 19.

28. Remini, *Andrew Jackson and the Course of American Empire*, 19–21.

29. Ibid.

30. Buchanan, *The Road to Guilford Courthouse*, 247–48; Tarleton quote, 247. Nadelhaft, *The Disorders of War*, 57. Weigley, *The Partisan War*, 22. Edgar and Bailey, *Biographical Directory of the South Carolina House of Representatives*, 2:557–58. McCrady, *The History of South Carolina in the Revolution, 1775–1780*, 816–17.

31. Howe, *History of the Presbyterian Church in South Carolina*, 1:483. Buchanan, *The Road to Guilford Courthouse*, 184–86. Ramsay, *History of South Carolina*, 1:215–16. Wickwire and Wickwire, *Cornwallis*, 178.

32. Howe, *History of the Presbyterian Church in South Carolina*, 1:481–84. Buchanan, *The Road to Guilford Courthouse*, 184–86. Ramsay, *History of South Carolina*, 1:215–16. Wickwire and Wickwire, *Cornwallis*, 178.

33. Rogers, *The History of Georgetown County*, 128–31; Tarleton quote, 129, 131. Nadelhaft, *The Disorders of War*, 57.

34. Wickwire and Wickwire, *Cornwallis*, 169–72; O'Hara quote, 170–71. Nadelhaft, *The Disorders of War*, 56–60. Lambert, *South Carolina Loyalists in the American Revolution*, 200.

35. Simms, *The Scout*, 12.

36. Weigley, *The Partisan War*, passim; Peter Paret and John W. Shy (*Guerrillas in the 1960s*) quote, 10.

37. Lambert, *South Carolina Loyalists in the American Revolution*, 183, 198–215; Cornwallis quote, 200.

38. Nadelhaft, *The Disorders of War*, 62–63. The average value of a slave was $2,700, multiplied by 25,000 slaves. Edgar, *South Carolina*, 80.

39. Francisco de Miranda quoted in Edgar, *South Carolina*, 244. Nadelhaft, *The Disorders of War*, 61.

40. Robert V. Remini, *Andrew Jackson* (New York: Perennial Library/Harper & Row, 1966), 18.

SEVEN

1. Lambert, *South Carolina Loyalists in the American Revolution*, 183–84, 198–215. McCrady, *The History of South Carolina in the Revolution, 1775–1780*, 573. Weigley, *The Partisan War*, 13–14. Pope, *The History of Newberry County*, 1:47. Higginbotham, *War of American Independence*, 360–64. Huff, *Greenville*, 26–27. Wickwire and Wickwire, *Cornwallis*, 145–46, 170. Buchanan, *The Road to Guilford Courthouse*, 123. Klein, *Unification of a Slave State*, 104. Nadelhaft, *The Disorders of War*, 45–69. Anne King Gregorie, *The History of Sumter County, South Carolina* (Sumter, SC: Library Board of Sumter County, 1954), 46.

2. Johnson, *Traditions and Reminiscences of the American Revolution in the South*, 339. Ramsay, *History of South Carolina*, 1:201. McCrady, *The History of South Carolina in the Revolution, 1775–1780*, 599–600. Wickwire and Wickwire, *Cornwallis*, 191. Bancroft, *History of the United States*, 10:313. Cornwallis quoted in Bass (*Ninety Six*), cited in Buchanan, *The Road to Guilford Courthouse*, 115.

3. McCrady, *The History of South Carolina in the Revolution, 1775–1780*, 852–53. McCrady, *The History of South Carolina in the Revolution, 1780–1783*, 744–47. Terry W. Lipscomb, *Revolutionary Battles, Skirmishes and Actions in South Carolina* (Columbia, SC: South Carolina Department of Archives and History, 1974), passim. Terry W. Lipscomb, "South Carolina Revolutionary

Battles: Part II," *Names in South Carolina* 21:23–27. Terry W. Lipscomb, "South Carolina Revolutionary Battles: Part III," *Names in South Carolina* 22:33–39. Terry W. Lipscomb, "South Carolina Revolutionary Battles: Part IV," *Names in South Carolina* 23:30–34. Terry W. Lipscomb, "South Carolina Revolutionary Battles: Part V," *Names in South Carolina* 24:13–19. Of the engagements in the lowcountry swamps, the British won only one (Waccamaw Neck); two were stalemates; and the rest were partisan triumphs.

4. McCrady, *The History of South Carolina in the Revolution, 1775–1780*, 853–54. McCrady, *The History of South Carolina in the Revolution, 1780–1783*, 746–47.

5. Clinton, *The American Rebellion*, 226. Wickwire and Wickwire, *Cornwallis*, 216, 227.

6. Wickwire and Wickwire, *Cornwallis*, 223.

7. Buchanan, *The Road to Guilford Courthouse*, 334. Wallace, *The History of South Carolina*, 2:258–91. McCrady, *The History of South Carolina in the Revolution, 1780–1783*, passim. Edgar, *South Carolina*, 238–44.

INDEX

———